EAST EUROPEAN NARRO
Written and Edited by KEITH C

The early morning train from Agnita has just arrived at Sibiu (Romania); motive power is an unidentified 0–8–0 built by the August 23 Works in 1949. September 1970.
Tony Eaton

CHANNEL VIEW PUBLICATIONS
Clevedon · Philadelphia · Adelaide

Outside Front Cover Top:
P.203 was one of the first narrow gauge 0–8–0s built by the Kolomna works in Russia. It eventually became no. E.70 of the Estonian State Railways. *Collection: Peeter Klaus*

Outside Front Cover Bottom:
CFR 0–8–0T no. 764.159 crosses the river Mureş near Cristeşti Mureş on 13 October 1969. *Werner Fritthum*

Back Cover:
The last narrow gauge passenger service scheduled for steam haulage in Europe is on the 750mm gauge Środa–Zaniemyśl line in western Poland. *Tony Eaton*

Library of Congress Cataloging-in-Publication Data
Chester, Keith.
East European Narrow Gauge / Keith Chester
1. Railroads, Narrow-gauge—Europe, Eastern
TF55.C46   1994
385′.52′0947–dc20   94-27118

British Library Cataloguing in Publication Data
A CIP catalogue record for this book is available from the British Library.

ISBN 1-873150-04-0

Channel View Publications
An imprint of Multilingual Matters Ltd.

UK: Frankfurt Lodge, Clevedon Hall, Victoria Road, Clevedon, Avon BS21 7SJ.
USA: 1900 Frost Road, Suite 101, Bristol, PA 19007, USA.
Australia: PO Box 6025, 83 Gilles Street, Adelaide, SA 5000, Australia.

Copyright © 1995 Keith Chester and authors of individual chapters

All rights reserved. No part of this work may be reproduced in any form or by any means without permission in writing from the publisher.

Typeset by Wayside Books, Clevedon, Avon.
Printed and bound in Great Britain by Amadeus Press Ltd, Huddersfield.

CONTENTS

Chapter No.		Page No.
	Introduction	3
	Abbreviations	4
1	Die Kleinbahn Des Kreises Jerichow I *Klaus Kieper*	5
2	Budapest Locomotive Factory Type 70 0–8–0T MÁV class 490 *Roland Beier*	15
3	The Upper Silesian Narrow Gauge Railway and its Steam Locomotives *Keith Chester*	25
4	The Kolomna 750mm Gauge 0–8–0s and their Years in Estonia *Peeter Klaus*	42
5	Forestry Railways in Jugoslavia *Keith Chester*	54
6	The Px48 0–8–0s of the PKP *Keith Chester*	60
7	The Hronec Forestry Railway *Keith Chester*	73
8	The Narrow Gauge Lines of the Romanian State Railways (CFR) *Şerban Lacriţeanu*	82
9	From the Iron to the Bamboo Curtain – a Narrow Gauge Survivor *Keith Chester, Peeter Klaus and Jeffrey Lanham*	95

INTRODUCTION

Probably the most momentous event of my lifetime was the collapse of communism in Eastern and Central Europe in 1989. Well I remember how, literally within days of the Velvet Revolution, Vienna suddenly filled with tour buses, bringing Czechs and Slovaks in their thousands to get their first glimpse of the 'West'.

But unlike most of those who had been caught on the wrong side of the ugly divide of postwar Europe, we 'Westerners' had at least been able to travel east before 1989, provided we were willing to pay sufficient hard currency and to put up with a grotesque bureaucracy.

And as the use of steam traction lasted much longer in the less efficient socialist economies, many railway enthusiasts were tempted to try their luck across the Iron Curtain. Given the attitude of the communist authorities to what they regarded as their 'strategic interests' – and railways clearly were so considered – it is not surprising that many enthusiasts found their visits somewhat problematic. Indeed there can be few of those who ventured east who do not have some story to tell of arrest, of film confiscated or of that precious worksplate smuggled across a border.

It would, however, be wrong to repeat the simplistic cliché of the Western media and talk of a monolithic 'Communist block', as if conditions had been the same everywhere within it. Attitudes to an interest in steam locos varied widely behind the so-called Iron Curtain. By the 1960s, the concept of railway enthusiast was well-established in the former GDR – even if the police could, when they felt so inclined, always find a reason to justify a short arrest or the occasional confiscation of film. On the other hand, Bulgaria never seemed to present any great problems, whilst Jugoslavia and Romania, which had been relatively 'easy' in the 1960s, became increasingly fraught in the 1970s.

By the 1980s we could not have visited the homes of the new friends we have since made from the TREN CLUBUL ROMAN without exposing them to a visit from Ceauşescu's *Securitate*. The USSR remained as suspicious of contacts with foreigners as ever and even during the period of *perestroika* Soviet railway enthusiasts were still being subjected to the attentions of the KGB.

Today much is changed. It is now certainly easier to walk around a loco shed in Romania or Poland than one in the UK; 'strategic' dumps are readily visited in the ex USSR. Yet of even greater interest and satisfaction has been the contact with railway enthusiasts in these countries. They had often pursued their interests in almost total isolation and frequently at some personal risk, painstakingly collecting material, both archival and photographic. Unfortunately the very nature of the conditions they had to work under meant that, although much was saved, much also was lost. Both the Chrzanów and Reşiţa lists, for example, are full of gaps and it is doubtful whether they shall ever be completed. That said, an enormous amount of material has survived and is only now beginning to filter west. This Special seeks to take advantage of this.

In addition to the authors, a great many people have contributed to this Special, answering obscure enquiries, correcting errors, as well as supplying information and photographs. To all of them, too many to mention personally, I extend my gratitude. I would, however, especially like to thank Messrs Roland Beier, Reimer Holzinger and Bogdan Pokropiński for their unfailing assistance in initially providing – and then checking – many of the loco lists in this Special. I also wish to acknowledge the help of my many students in Vienna who have willingly translated the strange texts about steam locomotives I have all too frequently presented them with. To everybody, thank you.

Finally sincere thanks to Donald Binns for first suggesting this Special and then supporting and encouraging me throughout its gestation.

It would, however, be as vain as it is foolish to pretend that the articles in this Special represent the final word on their subject or that, despite all our efforts, they are free of error. So much of value has already been destroyed, either wantonly or by accident, and although official archives in the region are slowly being made available, many questions remain unanswered. All contributors to this Special therefore welcome any corrections and additional material.

Keith Chester
Vienna, December 1993

ABBREVIATIONS

The following abbreviations are used to indicate locomotive builders:

AEG	Allgemeine Elektricitäts-Gesellschaft, Berlin-Hennigsdorf, Germany	Lokom	Lokomo Oy, Tampere, Finland
Arad	János Weitzer, Arad, Hungary	Maff	J.A.Maffei AG, Munich, Germany
BMAG	Berliner Maschinenbau AG (vorm. L. Schwartzkopff), Berlin, Germany	MÁVAG	Magyar Állami Vas-, Acél- és Gépgyárak, Budapest, Hungary
Bors	A. Borsig GmbH, Berlin-Tegel, Germany	O&K	Orenstein & Koppel AG, Berlin-Drewitz, Germany
Bp	Budapest Works, Budapest, Hungary; after 1945 MÁVAG	Pod	Podolsk, USSR
Chrz	Pierwsza Fabryka Lokomotyw w Polsce SA, Chrzanów, Poland; after 1945 Fablok	Res	Uzinele de Fer şi Domeniile din Reşiţa SA, Reşiţa, Romania
ČKD	Českomoravská-Kolben-Daněk A Sp, Prague, Czechoslovakia	Schw	Berliner Maschinenbau AG (vorm. L. Schwartzkopff), Berlin, Germany
Dav	Davenport Locomotive Works, Davenport, Ia., USA	Sigl	G. Sigl Lokomotiv-Fabrik, Wiener Neustadt, Austria
FB	Société Franco-Belge de Matériel de Chemins de Fer, La Croyère, Belgium	Škoda	Škoda-Werke, Plzeň, Czechoslovakia
Hag	Christian Hagans, Erfurt, Germany	SlBr	Đuro Đaković, Industrija Lokomotiva, Slavonski Brod, Yugoslavia
Hart	Maschinenfabrik Richard Hartmann, Chemnitz, Germany	StEG	Staats-Eisenbahn-Gesellschaft, Vienna, Austria
Hens	Henschel & Sohn, Cassel, Germany	Tam	Tampereen Pellava ja Rauta-Teollisuus Oy, Tampere, Finland
Jung	Arnold Jung Lokomotivfabrik GmbH, Jungenthal, Germany	U23A	Uzinele '23 August', Bucureşti, Romania; formerly Malaxa
Kolo	Kolomna Locomotive Works, Kolomna, USSR	VEB LOWA	formerly LKM Babelsberg
KrLi	Lokomotivfabrik Krauss & Comp, Linz, Austria	Votsk	Votkinsk Locomotive Works, USSR
KrMü	Lokomotivfabrik Krauss & Comp, Munich, Germany	War	Warszawska Spółką Akcyjną Budowy Parowozów, Warsaw, Poland
LKM Babelsberg	VEB Lokomotivbau Karl Marx, Potsdam-Babelsberg, GDR	WrN	AG der Lokomotiv-Fabrik vorm. G. Sigl, Wiener Neustadt, Austria

Other abbreviations used are as follows:

AEV	*Allami Erdei Vasutak*: State Forestry Railways (Hungary)	KPEV	*(königlich) Preußische Eisenbahn-Verwaltung*: Prussian State Railways
BHStB	*Bosnisch-Herzegowinische Staatsbahn*: Bosnia-Hercegovinian State Railway (1895–1906)	LVD	*Latvijas Valsts Dzelzsceli*: Latvian State Railways
CFF	*Căile Ferate Forestiere*: State Forestry Railways (Romania)	MÁV	*Magyar Államvasutak*: Hungarian State Railways
CFI	*Căile Ferate Industriale*: State Industrial Railways (Romania)	OEG	*Oberschlesische Eisenbahn-Gesellschaft*: Upper Silesian Railway Company
CFR	*Căile Ferate Române*: Romanian State Railways	OSB	*Oberschlesische Schmalspurbahnen*: Upper Silesian Narrow Gauge Railways
DOKP	*Dyrekcya Okregowa Kolei Państwowych*: Regional division of PKP	ÖStB	*Österreichische Staatsbahnen*: Austrian State Railways (1945–53)
DR	*Deutsche Reichsbahn*: GDR State Railway (1949–93)	PDI	*Produzece ze Drvna Industrija*: Timber Industries Enterprise (Yugoslavia)
DRB	*Deutsche Reichsbahn-Gesellschaft*: German State Railways (1920–45)	PKP	*Polskie Koleje Państwowe*: Polish State Railways
ČSD	*Československé Státní Dráhy*: Czechoslovakian State Railways	PLŽ	*Považská Lesná Želenica*: Waag Valley Forestry Railway, Liptovský Hrádok (Slovakia)
EVR	*Eesti Vabariigi Raudtee*: Estonian State Railways	PLB	*Pommersche Landesbahnen*: Provincial Railways of Pommerania
FS	*Ferrovie dello Stato*: Italian State Railways	RBD	*Reichsbahndirektion*: Regional division of DRB
GEV	*Görgényivölgyi Erdei Vasút*: Gurghiu Forestry Industries Railway (Hungary)	RüKB	*Rügensche Kleinbahn*: Rügen Island Railway
GVI	*Gazdasagi Vasutak Igazgatósága*: Directorate of Agricultural Railways (Hungary)	SŽ	*Slovenské Železnice*: Slovak Railways (1940–44)
HÉV	*Helyi Érdekü Vasutak rt.*: State Local Railway (Hungary)	SŽD	*Sovetskie Železnie Dorogi*: Soviet Railways
		SäStb	*Sächsische Staatsbahnen*: State Railways of Saxony
JŽ	*Jugoslovenske železnice*: Yugoslavian Railways (since 1953)	SHS	*Kraljevina Srba, Hrvata i Slovenaca*: Railways of the Kingdom of the Serbs, Croats & Slovenians (1918–27)
JDŽ	*Jugoslovenske državne železnice*: Yugoslavian State Railways (1929–53)	ŠIPAD	*Šumsko Industrijsko Preduzeće A.D.*: Forestry Industrial Co. (formerly Otto Steinbeis AG, Yugoslavia)
Kat	*Kattowitz*: Kattowitz division of KPEV	TCDD	*Türkiye Cümhuriyeti Devlet Demiryollari*: Turkish State Railways
KJ I	*Kleinbahn des Kreises Jerichow I*: Jerichow I District Railway	TCR	*Tren Clubul Roman*: Railway Society of Romania
kkHB	*kaiserlich-königliche Heeresbahn*: Imperial Austrian Military Railways	UNRRA	United Nations Relief and Rehabilitation Administration
kkStB	*kaiserlich-königliche österreichische Staatsbahnen*: Imperial Austrian State Railways	VR	*Valtíon Rautatiet*: Finnish State Railways
		ZOJE	*Zittau-Oybin-Jonsdorfer Eisenbahn*: Zittau-Oybin-Jonsdorf Railway

DIE KLEINBAHN DES KREISES JERICHOW I

Klaus Kieper

By the last quarter of the nineteenth century, the state of Prussia was criss-crossed by a dense network of railways. Yet prolific as the KPEV and its forerunners had been, many smaller and medium-sized towns still had no rail connections. At a time when a railway was seen as a stimulus to local economic growth and 'prestige', not having one implied at best stagnation or even decline.

The railway law of 1838 laid down strict criteria for the construction of railways by the state. For 'strategic' reasons, Bismarck opposed the construction of private lines and it was only after his fall in 1890 that legislation was initiated permitting the building of private 'local' railways. The 20 years following the passing of the *Kleinbahngesetz* (= local railway law) on 28 July 1892 were a period of feverish construction of local railways, both of standard and narrow gauges.

One such was that built in the Kreis Jerichow I. A *Kreis* was, and indeed still is, the local administrative unit in Germany. Jerichow I covered a relatively large area (60km by 30km), consisting of four towns and 95 communities. The economy was principally agricultural. The only railway in the *Kreis* was the 1,435mm gauge Magdeburg–Potsdam line, which skirted its northern boundary.

In the early 1890s, a 'Railway Committee' was formed in the *Kreis* to consider various proposals for a railway. A standard gauge line from Burg to Havelberg was turned down in 1893, as were moves by the Prussian army to build a 600mm line to serve the local military exercise areas. In 1894 it was finally decided to build a 750mm line from Burg to Brandenburg via Magdeburgerforth and Ziesar, with a branch from Burg to Groß Lübars. Construction began in May 1895. Although hopes had been entertained for an opening in the autumn of the same year, it was in fact nearly a year later, on 4 April 1896, when the first section (from Burg to Magdeburgerforth) was opened for traffic; by the following October the branch to Groß Lübars and the rest of the 'mainline' to Ziesars were in service. The planned extension to Brandenburg, although begun, was never completed, as there was considerable local opposition as well as difficulties in arranging a crossing with the KPEV line near Brandenburg.

On 29 April 1899 it was decided to extend the line from Groß Lübars to Gommern, via Loburg; at Gommern there was a sugar factory which promised to be a major source of revenue for the railway. Between Groß Lübars and Loburg, there already existed a 1,435mm gauge line (from Biederitz, opened in 1892) and here a third rail was laid. To allow standard gauge military trains to run as far as Altengrabow, where there was a large training area, the existing KJ I 750mm line was converted to dual gauge. 1,435mm gauge trains over this section were normally hauled by a KJ I loco, using a *Zwischenwagen* or intermediary wagon. It wasn't, however, until 20 April 1903 that the 750mm line to Gommern was opened throughout. As all other projected lines had in the meantime been abandoned, this now represented the full extent of the KJ I – 101.64km in length.

Unlike many of the *Klein-* and *Kreisbahnen* which were built in the wake of the 1892 *Kleinbahngesetz*, the KJ I was a profitable concern from the very beginning; between 1900 and the outbreak of war in 1914, both goods and passenger traffic doubled

Three generations of locos at Burg. From left to right: no. 18, ex-Schlawe; no. 14, (O&K 1924) and no. 2, the last surviving original Jung 0–6–0T. c. 1935.
Collection: Klaus Kieper

to 188,821 tonnes and 595,219 fares sold respectively. The principal freight carried was agricultural products (sugar beets, potatoes, etc), but also brown coal briquettes, fertilisers. There was also a sizeable military traffic.

After the boom years of World War I and the immediate years following it, traffic levels dropped perilously towards the end of the 1920s in the face of growing road competition and then the severe economic depression in Germany.

In 1926, just before the crisis broke, the decision was taken to regauge the line to 1,435mm. Negotiations on the financing, however, dragged on interminably and were ultimately overtaken first by the economic depression of 1928–33 and then by the re-armament programme secretly pursued by the Nazis, which soaked up any spare capital nationwide. Only in 1936 were these plans, which had become increasingly unrealistic, finally abandoned.

99 4643 (O&K 9682/1922) leaves Burg with an evening train. To the right of the loco is the 1944 Latvian built railcar VT 137 600.
Klaus Kieper

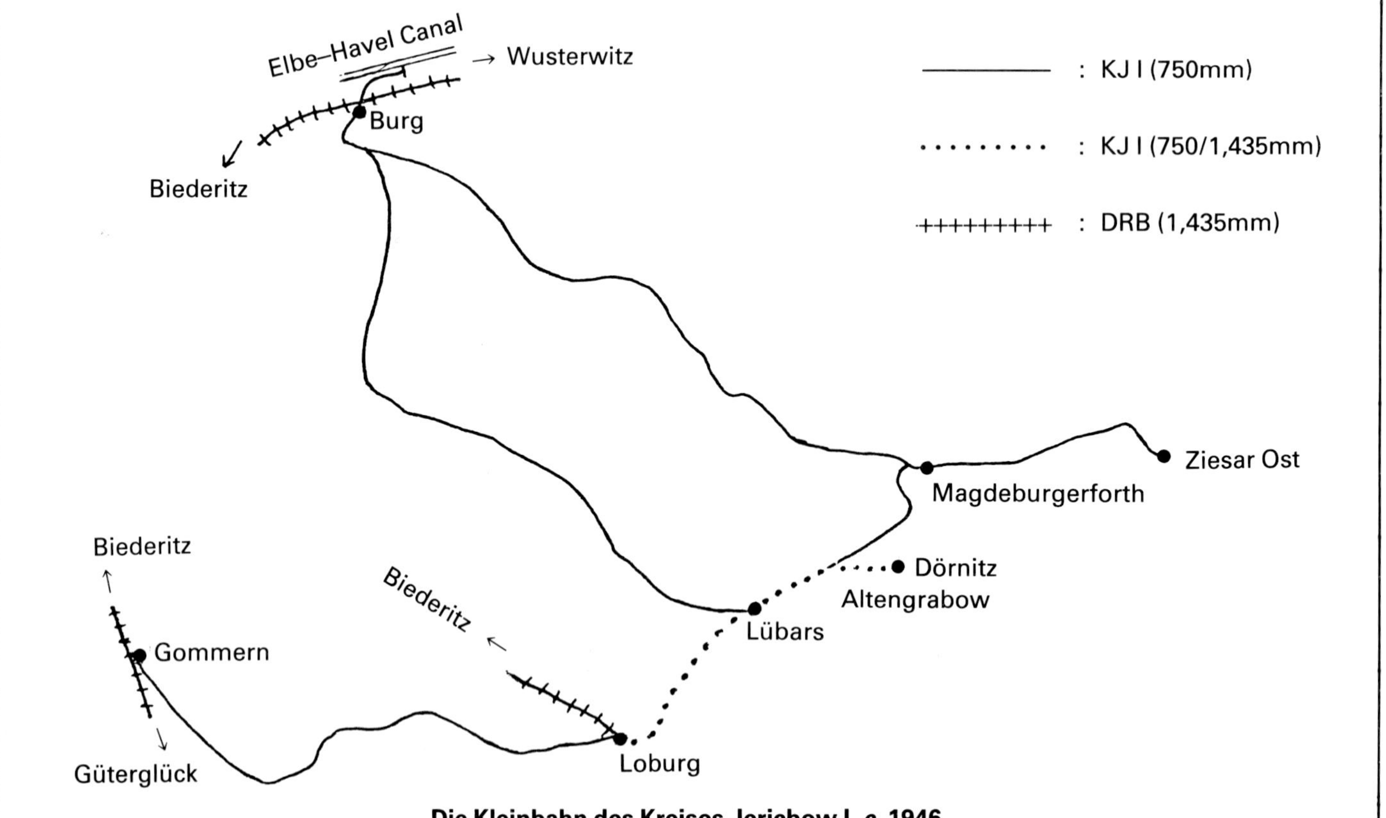

Die Kleinbahn des Kreises Jerichow I, c. 1946

The great irony was that the KJ I was shortly to benefit from this remilitarisation of Hitler's Germany. In the latter half of the 1930s, the railway began to carry increasing amounts of traffic, mostly stone and building materials in connection with the construction of *Autobahnen* and army barracks in the area. When war eventually broke out, munitions and other war materials were transhipped at Ziesar and proved to be another lucrative source of revenue.

Like most other railways, the KJ I survived World War II somewhat rundown, though it had suffered little physical damage. It was nationalised by the DR on 1 April 1949, together with nearly all other private railways in the Soviet Zone in Germany. The DR was chronically strapped for capital for investment and the KJ I was low on its list of priorities. Nevertheless, efforts were made in the 1950s to upgrade the track and to make the railway commercially more viable; but to no avail. Passenger traffic continued to be lost to the faster buses and lorries began to carry ever increasing amounts of the freight. Towards the end of the 1950s, modernisation of the railway (in the form of dieselisation and the introduction of *Rollwagen*) was briefly considered. But the writing was already on the wall and the KJ I was left untainted by 'progress'.

Passenger services between Loburg and Gommern were withdrawn on 2 May 1960, with freight following in stages in 1961–62. On 1 July 1965, Burg Mitte to Lübars was closed. The remaining section survived but 12 weeks and the final train on the KJ I ran on 25 September 1965.

To meet growing road competition head-on, the KJ I acquired two modern Mercedes Benz buses in 1934 and used them with some considerable success to replace poorly-frequented trains.
Collection: Klaus Kieper

In an attempt to win back traffic to the line, some desultory measures were taken in the late 1950s to modernise the KJ I, including the provision of this crane at Burg in 1956. Hitherto goods had been transhipped from standard to narrow gauge and vice-versa by hand. *Klaus Kieper*

99 4721 was not suitable for use on the 'mainline' of the KJ I and was restricted to shunting at Burg. It was destined to have the dubious privilege of hauling the track-lifting trains of the KJ I.   Klaus Kieper

THE LOCOMOTIVES OF THE KJ I

The first locomotives of the KJ I were five light 0–6–0Ts from Arnold Jung. Numbered 1–5, they were used in the construction of the line. Fitted with large spark arresters to their chimneys, they were nicknamed *Kaffeebrenner* or coffee-roasters. They successfully hauled all the traffic on the KJ I for the first five or six years of its existence.

In 1902 Hagans supplied three heavier 0–6–0Ts (KJ I nos 6–8) at the price of 16,500 Marks each. Immediately after their delivery it became evident that they were too heavy for the lightly laid lines of the KJ I. The solution was as simple as it was effective: the overflow pipe from the side water tanks was lowered by 150mm, thereby reducing the volume of water carried and the weight of the loco. When Hagans built two further locos for the KJ I in 1909 and 1910 (KJ I nos 9 & 10), the water tanks were correspondingly smaller.

Whilst this lessened damage to the permanent way, it raised certain operating difficulties, as the Hagans locos were heavy on water. Thus when the track was strengthened in the 1920s, the opportunity was taken to raise the overflow to its original level. Similarly when no. 7 was withdrawn in 1929, its larger side tanks were fitted to no. 9 to increase its water supply. No. 10, later 99 4615, however, retained its smaller tanks until withdrawn in 1956–57.

As things returned to normal after World War I, the KJ I purchased two 0–8–0Ts (nos 11 & 12) with inside frames and an enlarged firebox from O&K in 1922. Two years later O&K supplied a third identical 0–8–0T. This was numbered 14 to avoid 13!

The 1920s saw the KJ I in something of a cleft stick. On the one hand, rising levels of traffic required new motive power; on the other, the KJ I was hobbled by its plans to regauge, which had led to the decision not to acquire any new narrow gauge locos. Instead three secondhand O&K 0–8–0Ts were obtained from the Kleinbahn Landsberg-Rosenberg in Silesia, which had been converted to standard gauge in 1928. These had outside frames and flat slidebars; unfortunately the water capacity of these locos was even lower than that of the three O&Ks delivered in the early 1920s. They were numbered 15–17 and put into service on the KJ I between 1930 and 1934.

Of the three locos acquired from the Rosenberger Kleinbahn, the lightest, no. 17, was requisitioned by the Heeresfeldbahn in 1939 and eventually 'disappeared' in Poland. The other five O&K 0–8–0Ts bore for years the brunt of the work on the KJ I and all were taken over by the DR in 1949 becoming 99 4641–45.

During World War II, no. 11, later 99 4642, was rebuilt as a tender loco by the workshops at Burg. The side tanks were removed, the cab lengthened and a four-wheel tender provided. That this measure was taken should come as no surprise, as the KJ I was constantly beset by the problem of sufficient water supply for its locos on the relatively long sections they had to travel. Indeed it was quite common for the 0–8–0Ts to be coupled to an auxiliary tender. In 1956, 99 4642 was renumbered 99 4551. However, when it was rebuilt to a tank loco in 1959 – the conversion to an 0–8–0 was evidently not a happy one – it retained its new number (indicating a tender loco) until it was finally scrapped at Görlitz in May 1967.

No. 8 was the last of three 0–6–0Ts supplied to the KJ I in 1902 by Hagans of Erfurt. Heavy on water and thus unsuited to the relatively long runs on the railway, all had been withdrawn by 1929.
                              Collection: Uwe Bergmann

The KJ I purchased three 0–8–0Ts from O&K between 1922 and 1924. These had inside frames and, as can (just) be made out in this photograph of no. 14 taken at Burg, were fitted with long connecting rods, driving on the fourth axle. Collection: Klaus Kieper

Perversely, 99 4642/4551, which had been subjected to two rebuildings, was the only O&K 0–8–0T to more or less retain its original appearance. The other four 0–8–0Ts were all rebuilt by the DR between 1963 and 1965 as part of its *Rekonstruktionsprogramm*, designed to extend the life of its steam fleet. The reconstruction undertaken was a substantial one, with the locos receiving completely new, improved, boilers, a much altered cab and new side tanks.

It is doubtful whether the investment ever repaid itself. Upon the closure of the KJ I in the summer of 1965, the four *Rekoloks* were transferred away to the Prignitzerbahn. Here they saw little service. 99 4641 and 99 4645 were withdrawn after serious derailments in 1968 and 1969 respectively. 99 4643–44 were sent to Rügen in 1968, but again were little used on this Baltic Sea island.

Although plans for regauging were becoming increasingly unrealistic in the wake of the economic crisis of the 1930s, recourse was once again made to secondhand locos, this time with disastrous results. In 1934–35, the KJ I purchased two Krauss built 0–8–2Ts from the Schlawer Kleinbahn in Pommerania shortly after it was regauged to 1,435mm. Renumbered 18 and 19, neither loco proved successful on the KJ I and both were scrapped in 1938.

Following the failure of the two locos from Schlawe and the final decision not to rebuild the line, the KJ I was faced with an ageing fleet of locos at a time of rising traffic levels. Therefore in 1936, it ordered from Henschel & Sohn of Kassel two modern, superheated 2–8–0Ts, which it numbered 20 and 21. They survived the war to be taken over by the DR and were renumbered 99 4801–2 in 1950. The most modern and powerful locos on the KJ I, they formed the backbone of its motive power needs until it closed in 1965, whereupon they were transferred to the island of Rügen, where both are today (1993) still hard at work.

At the end of the 1940s, no. 21 was rebuilt to an 0–8–0 by the VEB LOWA. Although the loco does not seem to have been particularly successful in this form (it was considered a poor runner), it wasn't until 1964 that it reverted to a tank loco. That same year, both of the 2–8–0Ts received larger cabs and coal bunkers.

After World War II, two further locos were acquired by the KJ I, when like every other railway in Germany it urgently needed motive power. The first, which appeared on the line in April 1948, was a small 0–4–0T. Originally supplied by Henschel (works number 19514) in 1922 to Polinsky & Zöllner, this contractors locomotive had been extensively used in the building of *Autobahnen* in the 1930s. After some necessary modifications, it became KJ I no. 22 and was employed solely for shunting. The DR initially numbered it 99 4401, but it became 99 4721 in 1956. As such it was the last loco in service on the KJ I, being used for tracklifting in 1965–66. Today it is preserved in Halberstadt.

The final loco (no. 23) purchased by the KJ I as an independent concern was a small O&K 0–6–0T, originally supplied to the sugar factory at Gommern in 1920. Between 1949 and 1956, it was numbered 99 4402, before becoming 99 4301. Everything about this 0–6–0T, from its miniscule driving wheels (a mere 600mm) to its lack of anything other than a handbrake betrays its humble origins and not surprisingly it was restricted to shunting duties at Burg. Upon the closure of the line, it was sold to the nearby Ballerstedt-Transport-KG and used in its quarries until 1969. Since 1975 it has been plinthed in front of Gommern Station.

Outside framed KJ I no. 16 was originally constructed by O&K in 1912 for the Rosenberger Kreisbahn in Silesia; it was acquired by the KJ I in 1932 and photographed at Burg sometime in the 1930s.
Collection: Uwe Bergmann

Thirty years later, no. 16 had undergone a change in both ownership and shape, becoming 99 4641, a Rekolok of the DR. Ziesar 1965.
Klaus Kieper

99 4643 and 99 4645 were substantially rebuilt as part of the DR's Rekonstruktionsprogramm in the mid 1960s. In the process, the connecting rods were shortened and now drove on the third axle. 99 4643 is seen here at Burg in July 1965.
Klaus Kieper

Upon the closure of the KJ I in 1965, 99 4641, together with the three other surviving O&K 0–8–0Ts, was transferred to Prignitz. It is shown here at Perleberg.   Klaus Kieper

No. 1 of the Schlawer Kreisbahn (KrMü 4716/1902). Together with sister loco no. 2, this 0–8–2T, fitted with a Krauss-Helmholtz truck, was purchased secondhand in 1935. Neither lasted long on the KJ I, both being withdrawn in 1938.
Collection: Uwe Bergmann

When introduced in 1938, the two Henschel 2–8–0Ts were by far the most modern ng steam locos designed in Germany for a private railway. They bore a remarkable similarity to the three 2–8–2Ts O&K manufactured for the 900mm Bad Doberan–Kühlungsborn line in 1932.
Collection: Uwe Bergmann

Shortly before the closure of the KJ I, 99 4801 was photographed at Burg in August 1965. By that time the rivetted side tanks had been replaced by welded ones.   Klaus Kieper

A typical contractors loco, 99 4721 was much employed in the 1930s on the construction of Autobahnen *and other road schemes which ultimately were to sound the death knell for local railways like the KJ I. Burg, July 1965.   Klaus Kieper*

99 4301 was supplied to the sugar factory at Gommern in 1920 and only came to the KJ I after it was demolished in 1945–46. This small 0–6–0T was used principally on shunting duties at Burg. August 1965.   Klaus Kieper

After 1950, the DR transferred several other locos to the former KJ I, most on a temporary basis to ease motive power shortages. The loco which remained at Burg the longest was 99 4611. This small Jung 0–6–0T (works number 110 of 1891) had originally been delivered to the 785mm Brohltalbahn, one of the earliest narrow gauge railways in Germany. In 1942 it was regauged to 750mm and transferred to the Trusebahn in Thuringia. In 1958 it came to Burg where it was used on shunting duties. Although not officially withdrawn until 1966, 99 4611 didn't work after 1962. Other known transfers – none for any appreciable period of time – included Saxon Meyers 99 551, 574, 586 and 99 4541, a Podolsky 0–8–0 originally intended for a forestry railway in Romania.

Although strictly outside the remit of this article, brief mention should be made of the fact that the KJ I purchased an 80HP diesel from BMAG in 1937. Finally between 1963 and closure in 1965, the DR tried out a diesel railcar, built in Latvia in 1944, on the ex-KJ I in an attempt to stave off the inevitable. That it didn't says everything about both the railcar and the BMAG diesel.

The author wishes to acknowledge his debt to the researches of Hans Röper.

The Locomotives of the KJ I

KJ I	DR 1950	Wheels	Builder		Remarks
1	—	0–6–0T	Jung	232/1895	wd 1925
2	—	0–6–0T	Jung	233/1895	wd 1936
3	—	0–6–0T	Jung	234/1895	wd 1925
4	—	0–6–0T	Jung	254/1896	wd 1925
5	—	0–6–0T	Jung	272/1897	wd 1925
6	—	0–6–0T	Hag	468/1902	wd 1926
7	—	0–6–0T	Hag	469/1902	wd 1929
8	—	0–6–0T	Hag	470/1902	wd 1928
9	99 4614	0–6–0T	Hag	611/1909	wd 1963
10	99 4615	0–6–0T	Hag	651/1910	wd 1957
11	99 4642	0–8–0T	O&K	9681/1922	1956 99 4551; wd 1967
12	99 4643	0–8–0T	O&K	9682/1922	1964 *Rekolok*; 1966 Prignitz; 1968 Rügen
14	99 4645	0–8–0T	O&K	10862/1924	1965 *Rekolok*; 1966 Prignitz; wd 1968
15	99 4644	0–8–0T	O&K	10501/1923	1930 ex Rosenberger Krb; 1964 *Rekolok*; 1966 Prignitz; 1969 Rügen; pres Neustrelitz MPD
16	99 4641	0–8–0T	O&K	5216/1912	1932 ex Rosenberger Krb; 1963 *Rekolok*; 1966 Prignitz
17	—	0–8–0T	O&K	2235/1907	1929 ex Rosenberger Krb; 1944 Heeresfeldbahn
18	—	0–8–2T	KrMü	4716/1902	1935 ex Schlawer Kleinbahn 1"; wd 1938
19	—	0–8–2T	KrMü	5211/1904	1935 ex Schlawer Kleinbahn 2"; wd 1938
20	99 4801	2–8–0T	Hens	24367/1938	1966 Rügen; 1991 099 780
21	99 4802	2–8–0T	Hens	24368/1938	1966 Rügen; 1991 099 781
22	99 4721	0–4–0T	Hens	19514/1922	1948 ex Polinsky & Zöllner; 1949–56 99 4401; pres Halberstadt
23	99 4301	0–6–0T	O&K	9418/1920	1946(?) ex Gommern sugar factory; 1949–56 99 4402; 1966 Ballenstedt Transport KG; 1975 pres Gommern

Locomotives transferred to the former KJ I by the DR after 1949

99 551	0–4–4–0T	Hart	3204/1908
99 574	0–4–4–0T	Hart	3556/1912
99 586	0–4–4–0T	Hart	3606/1912
99 4541	0–8–0	Pod	0042/1934
99 4611	0–6–0T	Jung	110/1891

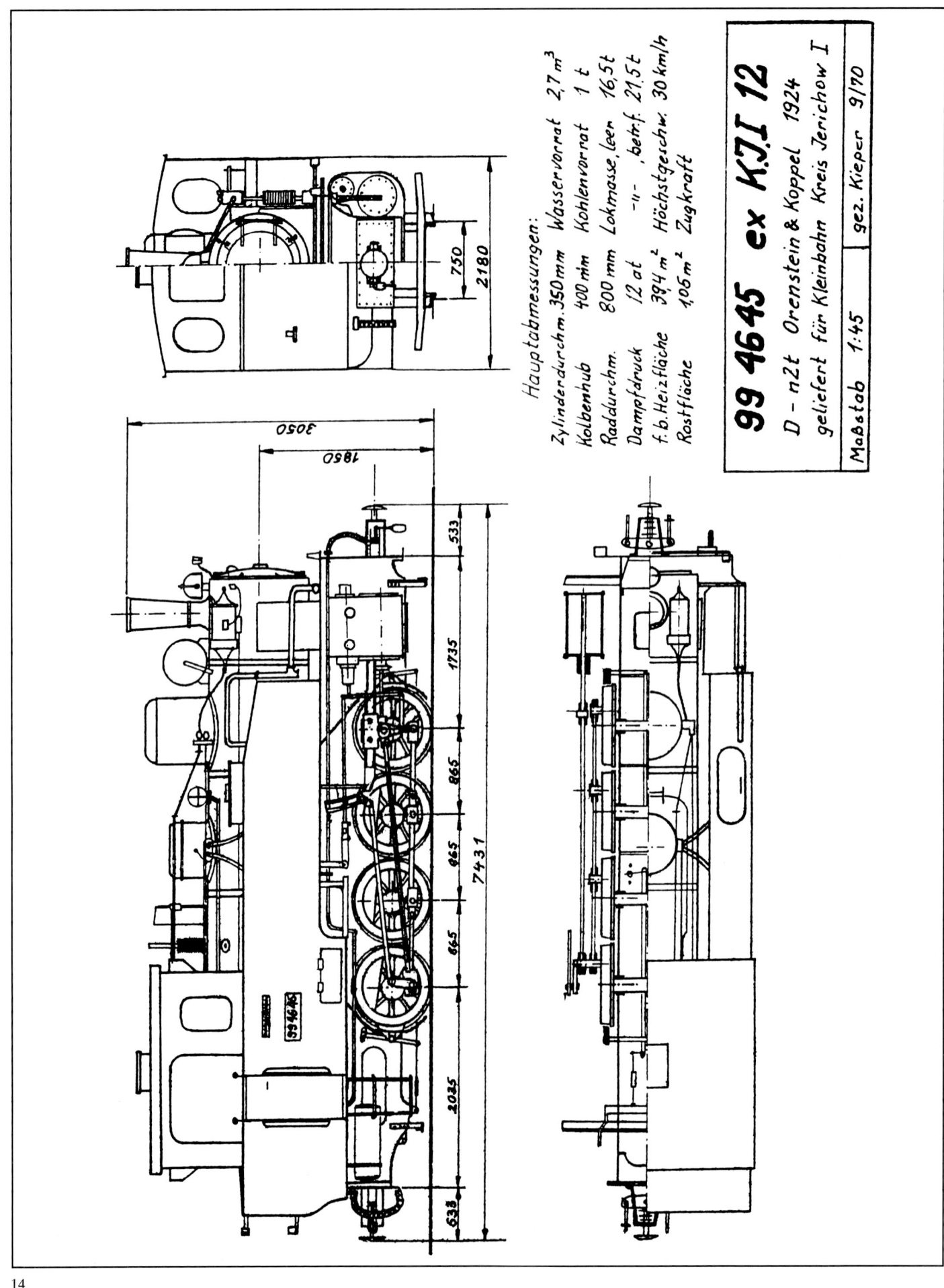

BUDAPEST LOCOMOTIVE FACTORY TYPE 70 0–8–0T MÁV CLASS 490

Roland Beier

2

The construction of narrow gauge locomotives in Hungary dates back to 1872, when the StEG subsidiary at Resicza, today better known as Reşiţa, manufactured a 950mm gauge 0–4–0T for use on the internal railway at its own works. Four years later, the Budapest factory produced its first narrow gauge loco, an 0–8–0T for the 790mm works railway at Salgotarjan steel works.

The great majority of Hungarian narrow gauge locos were, however, built for 760mm gauge – the 'standard' within the Monarchy. Most were supplied to privately-owned lines, but later the MÁV constructed its own lines to this gauge.

The most widely used narrow gauge locomotive on the MÁV was an 0–8–0T, class 490. It was built by the Bupadest factory between 1905 and 1950 virtually unaltered in 21 lots. The first locos of type 70, as it was originally designated by Budapest, were delivered to private railways in Transylvania, today Romania. The MÁV acquired its first two, which it classified as Category XXIc, for the Szatmár–Bikszádi (Satu Mare–Bixad) line, also in Transylvania. In the new numbering scheme, introduced by the MÁV in 1911, these 0–8–0Ts became class 490.

The Budapest type 70 was a two cylinder simple with Stephenson valve gear; it had outside frames and Klien-Lindner axles. This meant that the rigid wheelbase was only 1,150mm, as against a total one of 3,750mm. This permitted the type 70 to negotiate tight curves with great ease, a characteristic for which these locos were well known. Axle loadings were 5.5 tonnes, with the loco weighing 22t in working order. Water and coal capacity was 2m^3 and 1m^3 respectively. Maximum permitted speed was 35kmph. On the level this 290 HP loco could haul 210 tonnes at 25kmph. A total of 52 locos in the original version were delivered up to 1938.

By allying with the Axis powers, Hungary initially found itself on the winning side in World War II and regained much of Transylvania in 1940, which it had lost in 1918. Consequently the MÁV suddenly was faced with the need for new narrow gauge motive power, principally for its former 760mm lines in Transylvania, and it chose to build a further series of the proven 490. The new series differed from the original in several ways, notably in the provision of Heusinger-Walschaerts valve gear and an air brake. In addition, both water and coal capacity were increased, raising the weight in working order to 24 tonnes and thereby the axle loading to six.

A total of 90 locos were constructed to this improved design between 1942 and 1950. They were delivered to both the MÁV and numerous other customers.

Budapest works supplied the first 3 type 70s to the Gurghiu Forestry Industries Railway (GEV) in 1905; nearly 90 years later, the last active survivor of the class, CFF 764–348 (MÁVAG 5859/1950) was still at work on the same system. Lăpuşna, 7 April 1993.   *Keith Chester*

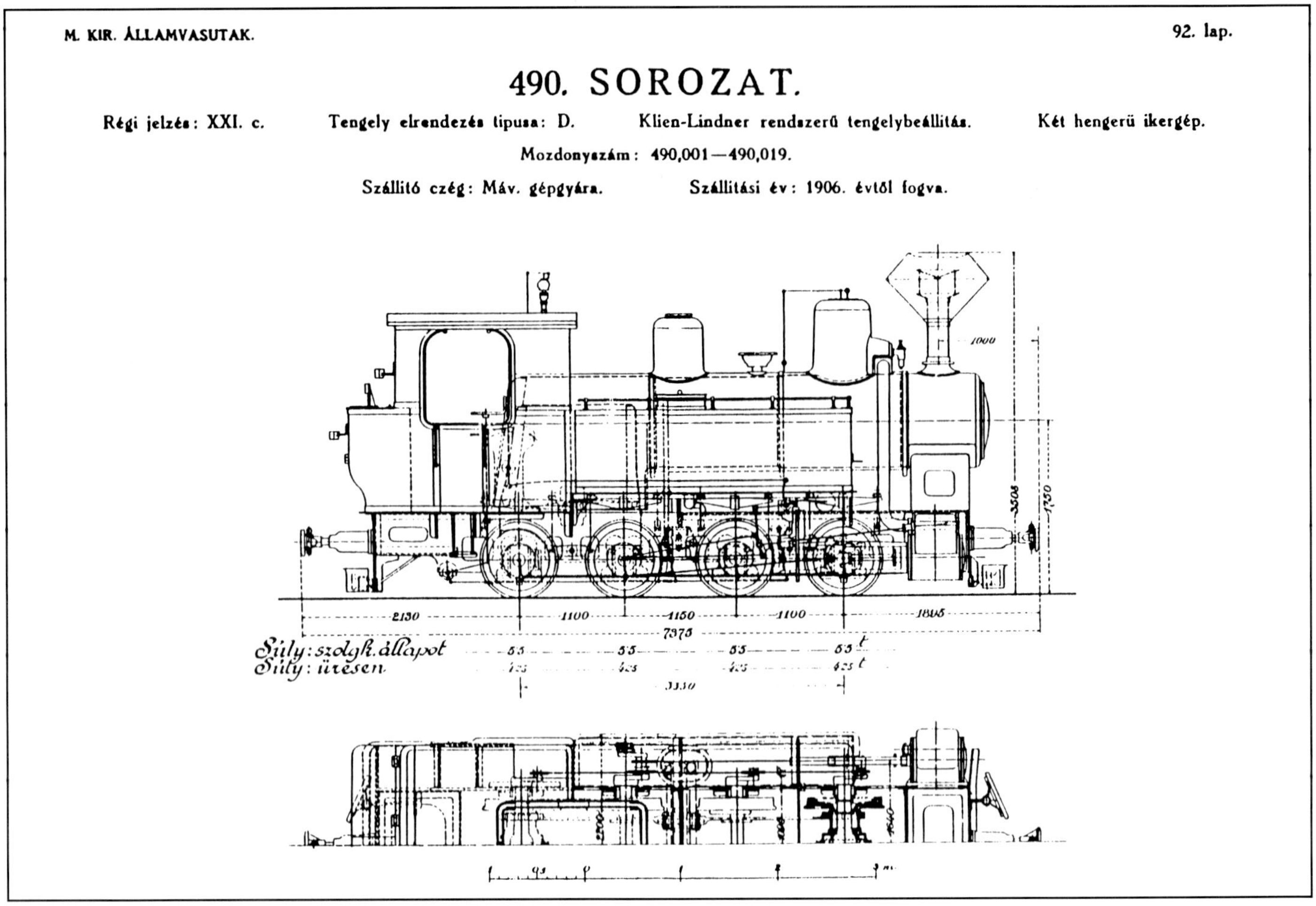
M. KIR. ÁLLAMVASUTAK.
92. lap.
490. SOROZAT.
Régi jelzés: XXI. c.
Tengely elrendezés tipusa: D.
Klien-Lindner rendszerű tengelybeállitás.
Két hengerü ikergép.
Mozdonyszám: 490,001—490,019.
Szállitó czég: Máv. gépgyára.
Szállitási év: 1906. évtől fogva.
2130
1100
1150
1100
1895
7375
Súly: szolgk. állapot
Súly: üresen.
3300
1000
3508
1750

HUNGARY

As already mentioned, the MÁV obtained its first 490s in 1906; by 1914, it had 31 in stock. Of these only two remained in (a much diminished) Hungary after 1918 and were given up to works railways in 1922. Some of the other locos had been loaned to the k.k. Heeresbahn (kkHB) in the course of World War I and they were used on various fronts by the armies of the Monarchy. With the cessation of hostilities, the surviving 490s were to be found in either Jugoslavia or Romania.

The fate of the eight 490s which had been supplied direct to the kkHB (490.951–58) was similar. After 1918, they were divided between Jugoslavia and the Republic of Czechoslovakia; two came into the stock of the FS and one to the PKP.

The remaining 13 locos built prior to 1914 were delivered to various private and works railways in Kingdom of Hungary. Some of these were also requisitioned by the kkHB and as a consequence were ultimately distributed among the successor states of the Austro-Hungarian Empire.

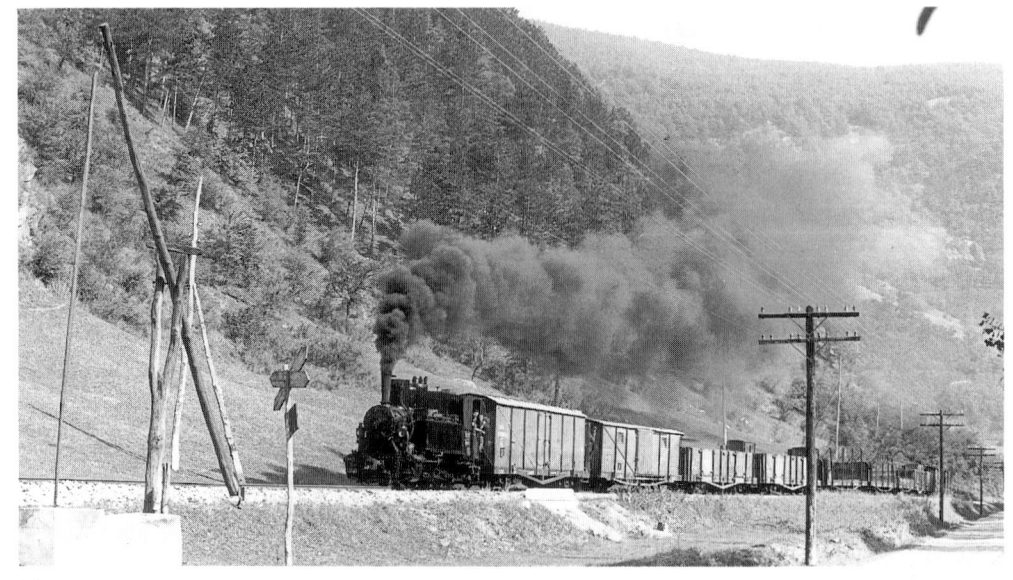

In the 1960s there was little evidence of 'progress' in rural Romania. Here 490.043 (Bp 5264/1942) heads a freight past a traditional well or fântînă. *Gerhard Luft*

The 5km mineral railway from Szob to the quarries at Márianosztra was home to the last four 490s in service in Hungary; with dieselisation just a few months away, 490,057 was photographed at Szob MPD on 5 April 1980. Keith Chester

In 1939–40 some locos returned to the MÁV and received their former numbers. Two locos, which had previously not been owned by the MÁV, were given the numbers 490,032 and 033. In 1942, 20 new locos were constructed for the MÁV and numbered 490,034–053. At the end of the war, just as in 1918, Hungary lost territories and the MÁV the greater part of its 490s – again mostly to Romania. Some, however, were taken over by the ČSD and the Soviet Union. In 1950 therefore, Budapest built a further eight 490s for the MÁV (490,054–061).

These locos were used on various narrow gauge railways in Hungary. Their final duties were on the freight only line between Szob and the quarries at Márianosztra, where they were in service until about mid 1980. Today several are preserved at various sites throughout Hungary; of these two are operational.

ROMANIA

The very first three locos of type 70 were supplied in 1905 to the *Görgényivölgyi Erdei Vasút* (or Gurghiu Forestry Industries Railway) in Transylvania as its nos 1–3. This line was nationalised in 1948 and thereafter was known as CFF Reghin. By a quirk of fate the last remaining 490 in commercial service (1993) can be found on the sole surviving stub of the Reghin system, the Lăpușna branch. Although the loco, 764–348, is one of the newer, enlarged series, the story of the class might indeed be said to have turned full circle.

After 1918 numerous 490s came into the stock of new Romanian owners, mostly the CFR, but also forestry and industrial railways. For its part, the CFR retained the MÁV numbers. Further locos were acquired after 1945 and in 1950, Budapest supplied 10 to the CFF as its 764–341, 347–355.

The CFF operated 17 type 70s over the years. 764–355 is seen here working a train along the Ihosa branch of CFF Vișeu de Sus, one of the last forestry lines to use these Budapest locos extensively. 3 April 1985. Keith Chester

The MÁV initially ordered type 70s for its 760mm lines in Transylvania and many of these were taken into the stock of the CFR after World War I when this became part of Romania. 490.014 (Bp 2854/1912) crosses a passenger train on the Turda system, 18 September 1966.
Trevor Rowe

JUGOSLAVIA

The first 490s were introduced into what was to become Jugoslavia by the kkHB during World War I. They were principally employed on the Steinbeisbahn. Most of these either remained on the Steinbeisbahn after 1918 or were taken into the stock of the newly-formed SHS, becoming JDŽ class 81 in 1933.

In 1942, 81–004 (MÁV 490,019) turned up briefly in Austria. It was in service on the Steiermärkische Landesbahnen as 0 40 until 1948, when it was returned to Jugoslavia.

In 1947, 20 490s were delivered to Jugoslavia, going mostly to forestry and works railways, though some were (nominally) allocated to the JDŽ, which used them on industrial lines. A further seven followed in 1949. The last of these locos worked at Banovici mine in Bosnia, until replaced by spare 0–8–2s of class 83. One was preserved at Banovici, though its present fate is unknown.

In 1947–49, Technopromet Beograd took delivery of 31 enlarged 490s, which were sent to various industrial and forestry lines in Yugoslavia. Nominally a JŽ loco, 5535 (MÁVAG 5535/1947) was photographed at Gračanica on 6 July 1964.
Alfred Luft

In 1953 the JDŽ became the JŽ, but six years later 81–006 was still carrying a JDŽ plate. Olovo, 10 August 1959.
Alfred Luft

By 1967 the driver of 81–006 (Bp 3155/1914) was less friendly. 'Ne može!' he is saying. 'No photographs!' Zavidoviči, 4 September 1967. Werner Fritthum

SLOVAKIA

Some MÁV 490s came into the stock of the ČSD after 1918 and were classified U45. In 1942, Budapest supplied two of the enlarged type 70 to the state forestry railways of the short-lived fascist Slovakian republic. These two locos, U46,901 and U46,902, and other type 70s, were used on various forestry railways in Slovakia and several have been preserved.

UKRAINE/SOVIET UNION

With the accession of Podkarpatská Rus (Ruthenia) to the USSR in 1945, some MÁV 490s also passed into Soviet ownership. They were used on the narrow gauge railway at Beregszász (Beregovo). Locos known to have worked here include 490,023, 030, 032, 033, 036 and 036. By 1955 they had all been replaced by the more modern and powerful 0–8–0s of class Gr, built by LKM Babelsberg as reparations. Other 490s were regauged to 750mm and used on various narrow gauge lines in the Soviet Union.

In 1944–45, ten 490s were under construction at the Budapest works. These were intended for the MÁV and would have become nos 490,054–063. Instead they were sent to the Soviet Union as reparations and were employed on various industrial lines there. Presumably they were first regauged to 750mm.

BULGARIA

In 1949 three locos of type 70 were imported to Bulgaria by Metalimpex Sofia. Unfortunately nothing is known of their subsequent fate.

*Two of the enlarged 490s went to Slovakia in the 1940s and worked on forestry railways there until the late 1960s. Shortly before closure, U46,902 heads a special on the forestry railway at Liptovský Hrádok. 1968.
Collection: Jiri Joachymstál*

The Budapest Locomotive Factory Type 70 0–8–0Ts: Locomotive List

1810/1905 GEV 1, 1948 → CFF 764–302
1811/1905 GEV 2, 1948 → CFF 764–303
1812/1905 GEV 3, 1941 → MÁV 490,101; 1945 → CFR; 1948 → CFF 764–304
1829/1905 Diósi Ignácz, Nagyvárad ALFRED; 1941 → MÁV 490,102; 1945 → CFR; 1948 → CFF 764–328
1846/1906 MÁV XXIc 6967; 1911 → 490,001; 1916 → Steinbeisbahn 33; 1918 → MÁV; 1922 → Gant bauxite works ROBERT
1847/1906 MÁV XXIc 6968; 1911 → 490,002; 1914 → kkHB; 1915 → MÁV; 1924 → CFR 490.002
2078/1908 MÁV XXIc 6969; 1911 → 490,003; 1914 → kkHB; 1917 → Steinbeisbahn 49; 1918 → SHS 490.003; → PDI Janj
2083/1908 MÁV XXIc 6970; 1911 → 490,004; 1914 → kkHB; 1915 → MÁV; 1918 → CFR 490.004
2178/1908 Diósi Ignácz, Nagyvárad BORISKA; 1941 → MÁV 490,103; 1945 → CFR 490.103
2501/1910 MÁV XXIc 6971; 1911 → 490,005; 1916 → Steinbeisbahn 34; 1920 → ŠIPAD 34
2502/1910 MÁV XXIc 6972; 1911 → 490,006; 1918 → CFR 490.006; 1941 → MÁV; 1945 → CFR
2847/1912 MÁV 490,007; 1914 → kkHB; 1914 → kkHB; 1916 → Steinbeisbahn 36; 1918 → SHS 490.007
2848/1912 MÁV 490,008; 1914 → kkHB; 1924 → CFR 490.008
2849/1912 MÁV 490,009; 1916 → Steinbeisbahn 31; 1924 → CFR 490.009
2850/1912 MÁV 490,010; 1916 → Steinbeisbahn; 1918 → SHS 490.010
2851/1912 MÁV 490,011; 1915 → kkHB; 1924 → CFR 490.011
2852/1912 MÁV 490,012; 1916 → kkHB; 1918 → CFR 490.012; 1940 → MÁV; 1945 → CFR
2853/1912 MÁV 490,013; 1914 → kkHB; 1916 → Steinbeisbahn; 1918 → SHS 490.013; 1933 → JDŽ 81–003
2854/1912 MÁV 490,014; 1914 → kkHB; 1918 → CFR 490.014
2861/1912 MÁV 490,015; 1915 → kkHB; 1918 → SHS 490.015; 1933 → JDŽ 81–001; 1941 → DRB 99 831; 1945 → ÖStB; 1947 → JDŽ
2862/1912 MÁV 490,016; 1916 → kkHB; 1918 → CFR 490.016
2863/1912 MÁV 490,017; 1918 → CFR 490.017
2864/1912 Nagyváradi Erdöipar Rt. Mezötelegd SZECHENYI; → La Roche és Darvas
3105/1912 MÁV 490,018; 1916 → Steinbeisbahn 35; 1918 → ŠIPAD 35
3106/1912 MÁV 490,019; 1915 → kkHB (Steinbeisbahn); 1918 → SHS 490.019; 1933 → JDŽ 81–004; 1941 → DRB 99 832; 1942 → StLB O 40; 1948 → JDŽ
3107/1912 Grantal sugar factory 6; 1916 → MÁV 490,959; 1915 → Steinbeisbahn 29; 1916 → kkHB; 1918 → Borsabahn 26, 1920 → ČSD U45001; 1939 → MÁV 490,032; 1945 → USSR
3108/1912 Grantal sugar factory 7; 1916 → MÁV 490,960; 1915 → Steinbeisbahn 30; 1918 → ŠIPAD 33
3109/1912 Grantal sugar factory 8; 1915 → MÁV 490,961; → Steinbeisbahn 32; 1918 → ŠIPAD 39
3110/1912 (MÁV) 490,951; 1915 → kkHB; 1918 → FS 4051
3153/1914 MÁV 490,020; 1914 → kkHB (Steinbeisbahn); 1918 → SHS 490.020; 1933 → JDŽ 81–005

Some of the Jugoslav type 70s received extended side tanks, which did little to improve their appearance. This photograph of 81–001 was taken at Olovo on 10 August 1959.
Alfred Luft

The Budapest Locomotive Factory Type 70 0–8–0Ts: Locomotive List *continued*

3154/1914 MÁV 490,021; 1915→ kkHB; 1924→ CFR 490.021
3155/1914 MÁV 490,022; 1914→ kkHB (Steinbeisbahn); 1918→ SHS 490.022; 1933→ JDŽ 81–006
3156/1914 MÁV 490,023; 1915→ kkHB; 1924→ CFR 490.023; 1940→ MÁV; 1944→ USSR
3157/1914 MÁV 490,024; 1914→ kkHB (Steinbeisbahn); 1918→ SHS 490.024; 1933→ JDŽ 81–002
3158/1914 MÁV 490,025; 1914→ kkHB; 1917→ Steinbeisbahn 50; 1918→ SHS 490.025; → Ljubija
3159/1914 MÁV 490,026; 1914→ kkHB; 1924→ CFR 490.026
3160/1914 MÁV 490,027; 1914→ kkHB; 1918→ CFR 490.027; 1940→ MÁV; 1944→ CFR
3161/1914 MÁV 490,028; 1924→ CFR 490.028
3162/1914 MÁV 490,029; 1922→ Gant bauxite works JOSZEF
3163/1914 MÁV 490,030; 1915→ kkHB; 1916→ MÁV; 1920→ Lillafüred forestry railway; 1942→ Busztyahaza forestry railway; 1944→ USSR
3164/1914 MÁV 490,031; 1916→ kkHB; 1918→ Steinbeisbahn 51; 1918→ SHS 490.031; → Prijedor
4271/1916 (MÁV) 490,952; 1916→ kkHB; 1918→ Roszahegy–Korytnica 4052; 1925→ ČSD U46001; 1927→ U45002; 1939→ MÁV 490,033; 1944→ USSR
4272/1916 (MÁV) 490,953; 1916→ kkHB; 1918→ FS 4053
4273/1916 (MÁV) 490,954; 1916→ kkHB; 1918→ Steinbeisbahn 52; → Prijedor
4274/1916 (MÁV) 490,955; 1916→ kkHB; 1918→ Steinbeisbahn 53; → Prijedor
4275/1916 (MÁV) 490,956; 1916→ kkHB; 1918→ PKP D8–1690; 1939→ DRB 99 2563; 1945→ DR 99 2563
4276/1916 (MÁV) 490,957; 1916→ kkHB; 1919→ SHS 12.026; 1933→ JDŽ 80–006
4277/1916 (MÁV) 490,958; 1916→ kkHB; 1919→ SHS 4058; 1933→ JDŽ 81–007
4680/1922 Keletmagyarországe erböketermalase Rt SUDRIC V; 1948→ CFF 764–313
4813/1923 Keletmagyarországe erböketermalase Rt SUDRIC VII; 1948→ CFF 764–318
4936/1926 Gant bauxite works 2 MARGIT
5171/1938 Gant bauxite works 3 MAGDA
5229/1942 Busztyahaza forestry railway no. 1; → K46913; 1944→ USSR
5230/1942 Busztyahaza forestry railway no. 2; → K46914; 1944→ USSR
5255/1942 MÁV 490,034; 1945→ Debrecen forestry railway no. 3; 1946→ MÁV; 1960→ GVI 490.034
5256/1942 MÁV 490,035; 1962 → GVI 490.035
5257/1942 MÁV 490,036; 1944→ USSR
5258/1942 MÁV 490,037; 1944→ USSR
5259/1942 MÁV 490,038; 1945→ DB; 1952→ MÁV
5260/1942 MÁV 490,039
5261/1942 MÁV 490,040; 1945→ CFR 490.040
5262/1942 MÁV 490,041; → Tapolca quarry
5263/1942 MÁV 490,042, 1944→ CFR, 1946→ USSR
5264/1942 MÁV 490,043; 1945→ CFR 490.043

81 004, seen here shunting the wood treatment plant at Vitez, was also fitted with extended tanks. 10 May 1971.   *Werner Fritthum*

The CFR Turda–Abrud line used a number of well-maintained 490s in the 1960s. As these four photos show, a lot could be achieved in one day, in this case 17 September 1965.

490.043 (Bp 5264/1942), an enlarged 490, near Lupşa.   *Alfred Luft*

Having taken water, 490.027 (Bp 3160/1914) awaits departure from Lupşa.   *Alfred Luft*

490.043 approaches Vidolm.
    Alfred Luft

490.043 later the same day
    Gerhard Luft

The Budapest Locomotive Factory Type 70 0–8–0Ts: Locomotive List *continued*

```
5265/1942   MÁV 490,044; 1959 → Oroszlany coal mine
5266/1942   MÁV 490,045; 1945 → CFR 490.045
5267/1942   MÁV 490,046; 1944 → CFR; 1946 → USSR
5268/1942   MÁV 490,047; 1944 → CFR; 1947 → USSR
5269/1942   MÁV 490,048; 1945 → CFR 490.048
5270/1942   MÁV 490,049
5271/1942   MÁV 490,050; 1945 → CFR 490.050
5272/1942   MÁV 490,051; 1945 → CFR 490.051
5273/1942   MÁV 490,052; 1944 → CFR; 1947 → USSR
5274/1942   MÁV 490,053
5275/1942   Ungvari Erböipar Gazdaság no. 1; 1944 → USSR
5276/1942   Gant bauxite works 5 IMRE
5277/1942   U46901; → Hronec forestry railway 6"
5278/1942   U45904; → Liptovský Hrádok forestry railway (PLŽ) U46902
5279/1942   Viseu forestry railway no. 5; 1945 → Lillafüred forestry railway no. 5; 1954 → AEV 467.601
5280/1942   Viseu forestry railway no. 6; 1945 → Lillafüred forestry railway no. 6; 1954 → AEV 467.602
5281/1942   GEV 6; 1948 → CFF 764–320
5282/1942   GEV 7; Ungvari Erböipar Gazdaság no. 11; 1945 → USSR
5443/1945   (MÁV 490,054) USSR
5444/1945   (MÁV 490,055) USSR
5445/1945   (MÁV 490,056) USSR
5446/1945   (MÁV 490,057) USSR
5447/1945   (MÁV 490,058) USSR
5448/1945   (MÁV 490,059) USSR
5449/1945   (MÁV 490,060) USSR
5450/1945   (MÁV 490,061) USSR
5451/1945   (MÁV 490,062) USSR
5452/1945   (MÁV 490,063) USSR
5533/1947   Technopromet Beograd for Zivnice; → Kladanj mine
5534/1947   Technopromet Beograd for PDI Janj; → PDI Grmeć; → PDI Drvar
5535/1947   Technopromet Beograd for JDŽ 55–35
5536/1947   Technopromet Beograd for JDŽ 55–36; → PDI Krivaja; → Zavidovići forestry railway
5592/1947   Jugometal for Zivnice; 1966 → Kladanj
5593/1947   Technopromet Beograd for JDŽ 55–93
```

Although Jugometal supplied 5595 to the JDŽ in 1947, the loco worked on forestry railways. The firebox is being cleaned at the end of the day at Usora on 11 August 1959.
Alfred Luft

The Budapest Locomotive Factory Type 70 0–8–0Ts: Locomotive List *continued*

5594/1947 Technopromet Beograd for Sebesic, Bila
5595/1947 Jugometal for JDŽ 55–95
5596/1947 Jugometal for JDŽ 55–96
5597/1947 Jugometal for Sebesic, Travnik
5598/1947 Jugometal for Banovici mine
5599/1947 Jugometal for Banovici mine
5600/1947 Technopromet Beograd for Zenica steelworks IX; → Zenica mine; → A.Lolic, Bila
5601/1947 Technopromet Beograd for Vares mine; → Zenica steelworks
5602/1947 Technopromet Beograd for Banovici mine
5603/1947 Technopromet Beograd for Banovici mine
5604/1947 Technopromet Beograd for Banovici mine
5605/1947 Technopromet Beograd for Banovici mine
5606/1947 Technopromet Beograd for Banovici mine
5607/1947 Technopromet Beograd for Vares mine; → PDI Konjuh; → Zagreb–Samobor no. 10; → Zenica steelworks no. X; → Kladanj
5666/1948 Technopromet Beograd for PDI Grmeć
5667/1948 Technopromet Beograd for Zivnice
5668/1948 Technopromet Beograd for Krivaja forestry railway; → Ribnica
5669/1948 Technopromet Beograd for Sebesic, Travnik
5670/1948 Technopromet Beograd for PDI Jahorina; → Zvijezda
5671/1948 Technopromet Beograd for PDI Janj; → Sipovo; → Bugojno
5672/1948 Technopromet Beograd
5673/1948 Technopromet Beograd
5674/1948 Technopromet Beograd
5675/1948 Technopromet Beograd
5839/1949 Technopromet Beograd for PDI Sana; → Kljuc
5840/1949 Technopromet Beograd for Krivaja forestry railway; → Stupcanica
5841/1949 Technopromet Beograd for PDI Konjuh; → Miljanovac; → Kladanj
5842/1949 Technopromet Beograd for Banovici mine
5843/1949 Technopromet Beograd for Banovici mine
5844/1949 Technopromet Beograd for Banovici mine
5845/1949 Technopromet Beograd for Banovici mine
5846/1950 MÁV 490,054
5847/1950 MÁV 490,055
5848/1950 MÁV 490,056; 196? GVI 490,056
5849/1950 MÁV 490,057; 1962 GVI 490,057
5850/1950 MÁV 490,058; 196? GVI 490,058
5851/1950 MÁV 490,059; → Tapolca quarry
5852/1950 MÁV 490,060; 1962 GVI 490,060
5853/1950 MÁV 490,061
5854/1950 Metalimpex Sofia
5855/1950 Bükkalja mine GYÖZÖ
5856/1950 Bükkalja; 1955 → GVI 490,081
5857/1950 Metalimpex Sofia
5858/1950 Metalimpex Sofia
5859/1950 Metalimport Bucureşti; → CFF 764–348
5860/1950 Metalimport Bucureşti; → CFF 764–351
5861/1950 Metalimport Bucureşti; → CFF 764–354
5862/1950 Metalimport Bucureşti; → CFF 764–355
5863/1950 Metalimport Bucureşti; → CFF 764–341
5864/1950 Metalimport Bucureşti; → CFF 764–347
5865/1950 Metalimport Bucureşti; → CFF 764–353
5866/1950 Metalimport Bucureşti; → CFF 764–350
5867/1950 Metalimport Bucureşti; → CFF 764–352
5868/1950 Metalimport Bucureşti; → CFF 764–349

THE UPPER SILESIAN NARROW GAUGE RAILWAY AND ITS STEAM LOCOMOTIVES

3

Keith Chester

Over the years the narrow gauge railway described here has been operated by various administrations and has also been known by a variety of different names in both German and Polish. In German it is generally called the 'Oberschlesische Schmalspurbahnen' (= The Upper Silesian Narrow Gauge Railways) and for convenience here this network of lines will be referred to as such, using the abbreviation OSB.

The area of Silesia is unique in Europe for both the extent and variety of the mineral deposits (principally coal and iron ore) beneath its soil. As early as the Middle Ages, it was home to a flourishing mining industry. Three particularly bloody wars were fought for control of its resources in the mid eighteenth century, which left much of the region, known as Upper Silesia, in Prussian hands. But whilst full-scale industrialisation in Germany is not normally considered to have taken place until after unification in 1871, in Silesia the process was well under way by the early and mid nineteenth century.

The first railway in Austria-Hungary was begun in 1835 to connect Vienna with Kraków and the vital coalfields in the Habsburg Silesian territories. The first line in Prussian Silesia was commenced in 1843 and by 1847 there was a through connection with Berlin and the ports of northern Germany. Rising demand for iron and steel products and improved means of transport led to the rapid industrialisation of the area in the mid nineteenth century.

The concession to build a 785mm narrow gauge railway connecting the various coalmines and steelworks in Upper Silesia and the mainline railways in the area was granted to the privately-owned Oberschlesische Eisenbahn-Gesellschaft on 24 March 1851. The OEG, which already operated a considerable network of standard gauge lines in Upper Silesia, commenced the construction of the 785mm line the same year. (The choice of gauge was actually not so unusual as it may seem, but in fact represented 30 Prussian *Zoll*). By 1857, the 'mainline' between Tarnowitz and Kunigundeweiche (later Kattowitz) was complete. With its numerous branches and sidings, the original line was over 90km long.

Initially the railway was operated using horses on the branches and sidings and 10 2–4–2Ts acquired from Günther of Wiener Neustadt in 1855–56 on the mainline. That the Prussians with a well-established locomotive industry of their own should have turned to the Austrians for motive power is perhaps not so surprising as it first looks. Günther was at this time developing the first narrow gauge locos built in Europe. These were for the 'Akademie Bau' at Wiener Neustadt and the Lambach–Gmunden line in Upper Austria (part of the Linz–Budweis horse tramway, for which, incidentally, locomotive traction had been proposed as early as 1826–27).

Just as in Austria, using horses and locomotives together proved to be a highly unsatisfactory combination on the OSB and the company soon decided to dispose of the horses. In 1856 it leased the horse operations to the contractor Pringsheim, whose firm was to be closely connected with the railway for the next 50 years. The OSB continued to run the Günther 2–4–2Ts on its mainline. It had little joy with these rather complicated locos and

The Tw47s and Tw53s were the final steam loco type developed for the Upper Silesian 785mm gauge lines. Here Tw53-2568 is to be seen at Bytom Karb MPD. May 1974.
Klaus Kieper

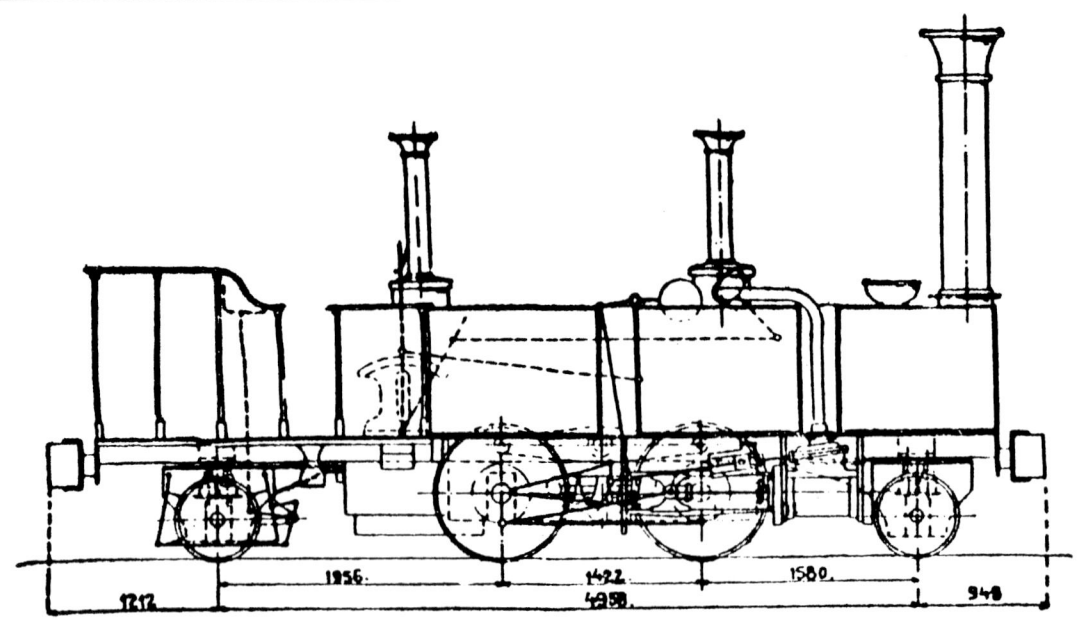

This drawing, reproduced from the September 1933 edition of Die Lokomotive, *is supposed to be of the 2–4–2Ts built by Günther for the Akadamie Bau at Wiener Neustadt in 1854–55. The origins of the drawing are, however, unclear and, as its dimensions do not entirely agree with those given for the locos which worked in Lower Austria, it may be speculated that in fact it shows the locos which were delivered to Upper Silesia. Whether or not this is the case, it can be reasonably assumed that the two designs were similar.*

experienced increasing difficulties and costs in operating them. Not surprisingly, the rebuilding of the line to standard gauge was mooted in the late 1850s. These plans were, however, abandoned before long, partly for financial reasons and partly because it was realised that a 1,435mm gauge line would be impracticable for the sharp curves (of which more below) to be found on the OSB. It must therefore have been with some relief that the OSB acceded to the wily Pringsheim's suggestion of giving up the use of steam traction and of granting his company a contract to provide motive power for the entire railway. A 12-year contract to this effect was signed on 1 October 1860. The steam locos quickly disappeared and were all sold in 1862–63. Thereafter the line was completely horse operated.

Horses, however, could not offer any long term solution; within 10 years they were no longer able to cope with the steadily rising levels of traffic. When Pringsheim's contract was renewed in 1872, the decision was taken to reintroduce steam locos. In 1884 the Oberschlesische Eisenbahn-Gesellschaft, which had been nationalised in 1856, was finally absorbed into the KPEV. Nevertheless, Pringsheim was granted the same year a new lease to operate the railway for a further ten years. This was renewed for what turned out to be the last time in 1894.

In 1923 BMAG supplied five 0–10–0Ts with the Czeczott system of articulation to Poland as reparations. When photographed at Bytom-Macekowice in May 1974, Tw9–2462 was already in store.

Klaus Kieper

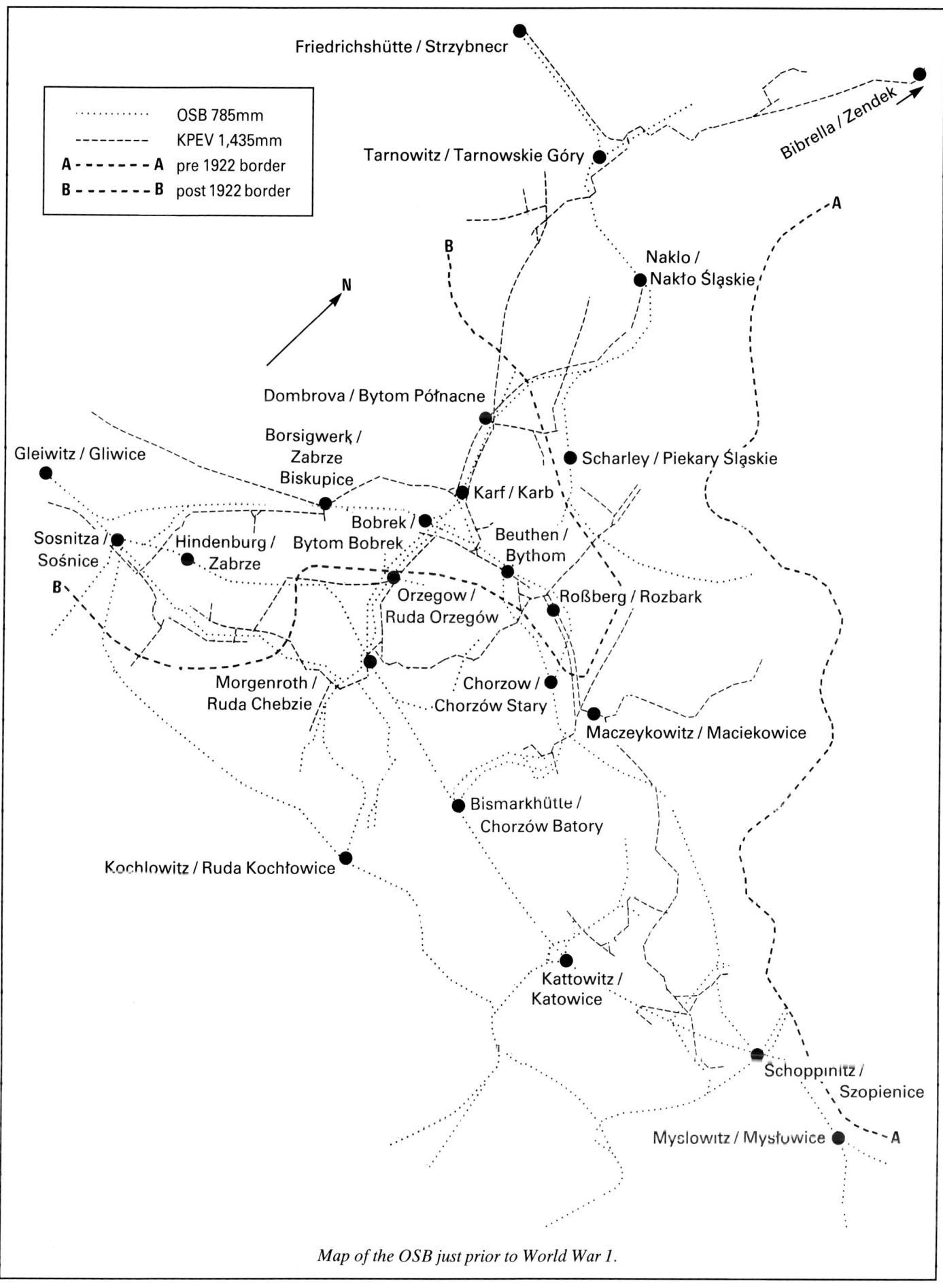

Map of the OSB just prior to World War 1.

99 420 was one of 11 T38s which came to the DRB after the division of the railway in 1922. Unlike their Polish counterparts, most of which survived World War II, all had been withdrawn by 1942.
Collection: Uwe Bergmann

A Borsig 0–6–2T, no. 5 of the Kleinbahn Gleiwitz-Rauden-Ratibor, is seen here shunting a train of standard gauge wagons on Rollböcke *at Gleiwitz-Trynek.*
Collection: Uwe Bergmann

In 1901 Pringsheim was operating 51 locomotives and had 755 employees; a further 151 people were employed by the KPEV Direktion in Kattowitz to administer the railway. By this time, the OSB had grown to a total length of 157.51km and connected no less than 163 mines and works with each other and the KPEV.

Following the attempt in 1900 of a consortium of industrialists to buy the OSB, the Prussian state, alive to the economic and strategic importance of the railway, decided to take it over completely; Pringsheim's contract was therefore not renewed in 1904. In addition to bringing some hitherto privately-owned lines and loading points under state control, the KPEV also acquired 55 locomotives from Pringsheim. With effect from 12 July 1904, the KPEV Direktion Kattowitz became responsible for all operations on the OSB and the railway greatly benefited both from having a single management and from the co-ordination of narrow and standard gauge operations.

In addition, the energetic management of the line by Geheimrat Stambke in the following 10 years led to booming levels of traffic (even to the introduction of a limited number of passenger services). As a consequence of this, many new lines were projected in the years prior to World War I. The most ambitious of these was a 50km extension joining the OSB with the River Oder at Cosel. None of these projects, however, came to fruition because of the outbreak of war.

The Great War was, to say the least, a difficult time for the OSB. On the one hand, the demands of the Silesian armaments industry saw traffic growing to unprecedented levels; on the other, the railway was obliged to supply locos and rolling stock to the Heeresfeldbahn – not all of which were returned at the end of hostilities. The OSB was thus frequently compelled to borrow locomotives from the nearby independent Kleinbahn from Gleiwitz to Ratibor (see below) and even from some of the works railways it served. Not until 1917–18 with the arrival of sufficient numbers of the powerful superheated 0–8–0Ts of class T38 was the motive power shortage eased.

But if the war had been difficult for the OSB, its aftermath was catastrophic. At Versailles, the victorious Allied powers confirmed the establishment of the independent Polish republic, which had been declared in November 1918. Allied troops occupied the economically vital region of Silesia, prior to the holding of a plebiscite over its future. Tensions as to whether Silesia should fall to Germany or Poland were greatly exacerbated by the fact that the territory's population was mixed; seeing how important the area would be to what was otherwise essentially an agricultural state, the Poles provoked three uprisings in Silesia between 1919 and 1921.

The plebiscite of March 1921 was inconclusive; the rural population voted overwhelmingly for Poland (40%), the towns

Something of a mystery: the number plate reads T31¹–2511, but the loco is clearly a T31. The PKP plate suggests the photo was taken in the mid 1920s.
Collection: Bogdan Pokropiński

An unidentified Pxu heading a Gliwice-Rudy passenger train in 1956. The 'u' indicates that the locos originally came from UNRRA.
Collection: Bogdan Pokropiński

for Germany (60%). The Allies were thus left with the unsavoury task of dividing Silesia. Much of it remained German, but two-thirds of its resources and industry went to Poland.

In turn this necessitated the division of the OSB; again Poland received two thirds. As of 18 June 1922, the Polish part of the railway, now known as the *Górnośląskie Koleje Dojazdowe*, was administered by the Katowice Division of the newly-formed PKP. The German third became part of the Oppeln Direktion of the DRB. The Poles received 41 locos and 3,398 wagons, the Germans 29 locos and 2,424 wagons. Unlike the locomotives, the wagons were pooled until 1937; the Polish ones were marked *Górny Śląsk*, and the German ones *Oberschlesien* (both translate as Upper Silesia). However, when the DRB ordered 847 new wagons in the 1920s, they bore the legend *Deutsche Reichsbahn* and were not permitted to be used on the PKP.

As may be imagined, the consequences of the division of such a highly integrated and densely operated network of lines were disastrous. There were no fewer than five official border crossings. Bureaucratic controls and nationalistic antipathy (*cf.* the DRB's refusal to pool its new wagons) led to inevitable delays and with the construction of new avoiding lines on both the Polish and German sides, cross-border and corridor traffic rapidly diminished. Ever increasing customs duties and tariffs imposed in both countries only served to further hamper traffic – as indeed they were intended to do. As part of the DRB, the railway struggled to cover its costs for the entire period between the two world wars. Between 1925 and 1929, that is even before the Crash of 1929, which hit Germany so hard, the number of staff employed by the DRB on the OSB was slashed from 627 to 380.

After Hitler's attack on Poland on 1 September 1939, (provoked, not coincidentally, on the Silesian border), the OSB was once again in German hands and for the next five and a half years (instead of the 1,000 prophesised by Hitler) was operated as a single unit by the Reichsbahndirektion Oppeln. At this time, the

After World War II the PKP built two series of 0–10–0Ts for use in Silesia. Tw47–2554 (Chrz 1674/ 1947) was photographed at Bytom in May 1974. Note the square buffers.
Klaus Kieper

railway had a total length of 193.9km. In 1942 all the former PKP locos were renumbered into the DRB system.

Upper Silesia was occupied by Soviet troops at the beginning of February 1945. The very speed of their advance meant that the Germans had had no time to systematically destroy the plant and infrastructure of the area; thus like most of the industry of Upper Silesia, the OSB survived World War II more or less intact, though very rundown.

A second Polish republic was established in 1945 and once again the German border was moved westwards – this time substantially – to the so-called Oder–Neisse line. All of Upper Silesia was now Polish and the OSB operated by the re-formed PKP alone. Shortly after the war, the hitherto separately owned and operated 785mm lines of the Gleiwitz-Ratibor Kleinbahn were also fully integrated into the OSB.

Over the past 45 years, the system has remained a key link, albeit a gradually contracting one, in the transportation network of Upper Silesia. Dieselisation was more or less completed by 1980, which in itself is indicative of the importance the Poles attached to these narrow gauge lines. How much, if any, of the OSB will survive after the shakedown following Poland's moves to a market economy at the beginning of the 1990s remains to be seen.

KLEINBAHN GLEIWITZ-RAUDEN-RATIBOR

This 47km long local line, with the gauge of 785mm, was opened in stages between 1899 and 1908 by the Oberschlesischen Dampfstraßenbahn (= Upper Silesian Steam Tramway), which had been active in the area since 1894. Within a few years, the tramway company was bought out by a bank consortium.

After the division of Silesia in 1922, the Kleinbahn remained in Germany. In 1926 it became part of the newly-formed Oberschlesische Überlandbahn and in 1928 part of the Verkehrsbetriebe Oberschlesien AG. When all of Silesia became Polish in 1945 following the German defeat, the line was absorbed into the PKP. Although the Kleinbahn had always had a connection with the OSB at Gleiwitz, it was only now, after 1945, that steps were taken to fully integrate its operations into those of the larger system.

Heavy flooding in July 1939 saw the temporary closure of the 1.6km section between Ratibor Rybniker Straße and Ratibor-Siemens. Lack of money and then the outbreak of war meant that this section was never restored to traffic and thereafter passengers wishing to make the connection between the main-line station at Ratibor (after 1945 Racibórz) and the narrow gauge railway were confronted with a walk of 35 minutes! The PKP regauged the last three kms of the Kleinbahn to 1,435mm

No. 7 was a chunky 0–8–0T supplied by Borsig (works number 10355) to the Kleinbahn in 1919.
Collection: Uwe Bergmann

AEG built two superheated 0–10–0Ts for freight duties on the Kleinbahn in 1925. To provide a flexible wheelbase, the first and fifth axles had a sideplay of 20mm and the middle one a reduced profile. No. 9, illustrated here, became PKP Tw9–2466 in 1961.
   Collection: Uwe Bergmann

and in part provided the narrow gauge line with a new formation. In latter years passenger services only operated between Gliwice (Gleiwitz) and Rudy (Rauden). Total closure of the railway is reported to have taken place in November 1991.

In addition to using various tram locos of the Oberschlesische Dampfstraßenbahn, the Kleinbahn acquired the following steam locomotives:

1	0–6–2T	Borsig	5368/1904	Txb2–2201	Sold 1956
2			5369/1904		
3			5370/1904	—	
4			5371/1904	Txb2–2202	Sold 1956
5			6279/1907	Txb2–2203	
6			6280/1907	Txb2–2204	
7	0–8–0T		10355/1919	—	
8	0–10–0T	AEG	2898/1925	Tw5–2601	(1947)
				Tw9–2466	(1961)
9			2899/1925	Tw5–2602	

Only the two AEG 0–10–0Ts were superheated. In 1926 AEG supplied two petrol-driven railcars and thereafter steam was limited to freight workings. As the war came to an end, the Germans stored all the serviceable steam locos at Lukasine. Some of them were put back into service by the PKP and two were sold to collieries in 1956. Passenger trains were once again steam hauled; dieselisation finally took place in 1970.

STEAM LOCOMOTIVES OF THE OSB
Günther 2–4–2Ts
The first locos supplied to the OSB were ten 2–4–2Ts, constructed by Günther of Wiener Neustadt in 1855–56. The solution of the Austrian engineers to the problem of providing the loco with a sufficiently flexible wheelbase was the use of hollow axles. These produced a loco which could negotiate the sharp curves of the OSB with ease. However, the short wheelbase of the rigid coupled axles meant that the loco was prone to rolling. A further difficulty was the fact that the hollow axles had no self-centering mechanism.

Not surprisingly these rather unsatisfactory and troublesome locomotives had a short life on the OSB; indeed they may be said to have been directly responsible for the what now seems extraordinary decision taken in 1860 to abandon locomotive haulage. The 10 locos were all sold in 1862–63 to various concerns; one is known to have worked on the Faxe Kalbruk railway in Denmark, where it became its no. 1.

Locomotives of the OSB

Günther 2–4–2T

1	Günther	145/1855
2		150/1855
3		176/1856
4		177/1856
5		178/1856
6		179/1856
7		206/1856
8		207/1856
9		208/1856
10		209/1856

Two locos sold in 1862; eight in 1863; one to Faxe Kalbruk, Denmark.

The Hagans and Krauss 0–4–0WTs
Seventeen of these 0–4–0WTs were built by Hagans (6) and Krauss, München (11) between 1872 and 1875, following the reintroduction of locomotives in 1872. They were fitted with Crompton style boilers and Allen valve gear. Coal was carried in small bunkers either side of the cab. Coal capacity was 0.45t and water 1.2m³. Five of the Hagans locos survived to become absorbed into the KPEV in 1904. The original loco (Hagans no. 1 and OSB no. 11) was sold to the Sächsische Staatseisenbahn in 1882. It was regauged to 750mm and received the classification 'Hg VII TK'. It was renumbered 'Zittau 5', but should not be confused with the 0–4–0T (type 1 K) of the same number and name of the privately-owned ZOJE. 'Zittau 5' worked on the Mügeln system of lines, before being withdrawn in 1896 and sold for industrial use the following year.

This was the very first loco built by Hagans and the first used by the OSB following the reintroduction of locomotive traction in 1872. All traffic was in the hands of these miniscule 0–4–0WTs until 1875.
Collection: Uwe Bergmann

Class T31 (0–6–0WT)

The 0–4–0WTs of 1872 soon proved to be unsuitable for the growing tonnages now being hauled along the 'mainline' of the OSB. In 1875 Krauss, München produced the first of 22 short wheelbased 0–6–0WTs of typical German design. Acquired in annual batches between 1875 and 1880, all were built by Krauss, save four from Hagans. Ten were taken over by the KPEV in 1904 and became class T31. An unknown number of them were commandeered by the Heeresfeldbahn during World War I and never returned. Together with locos sold and withdrawn (before 1914) this meant that only four T31s remained active on the books of the OSB in 1918. In the DRB renumbering scheme of 1925, they were allocated the numbers 99 7401–4, but all were withdrawn before receiving them.

Class T31[1] (0–6–0T)

Between 1884 and 1899, Krauss, München constructed 28 0–6–0Ts of an improved design for use on the OSB. The KPEV classified them as class T31[1]. All remained in Silesia on the OSB during the World War I. Withdrawals were heavy between 1918 and 1922, by which time only 13 remained in service. Three were allocated numbers in the new DRB scheme (99 7411–3), but only no. 60 survived long enough to actually carry one – 99 7411. The PKP is said to have taken seven (or 10) T31[1]s into stock, but precise details are lacking.

Locomotives of the OSB *continued*			
0–4–0WT			
11	Hag	1/1872	1882 to SäStb (Hg V11 TK: Zittau 5)
12		2/1872	Kat 12
13		4/1872	13
14		5/1872	14
15		8/1872	15
16		10/1872	16
1"	KrMü	189/1872	
2"		233/1872	
3"		234/1872	
4"		235/1872	
5"		240/1873	
6"		241/1873	
7"		242/1873	
8"		276/1873	
9"		393/1874	
10"		394/1874	
17		451/1875	

22 of these small 0–6–0WTs, subsequently classified T31 by the KPEV, were constructed by Krauss, München and Hagans between 1875 and 1880. No 32 emerged from the Hagans factory at Erfurt in 1877, works number 77.
Collection: Uwe Bergmann

Though larger than the T31s, the T31¹'s were by the mid 1890s increasingly underpowered and all had relatively short lives. No. 61 was allocated 99 7412 by the DRB in 1925, but never actually carried this number.
　　Collection: Uwe Bergmann

Class T36 (0–10–0T)

From its earliest days, the OSB was beset with a fundamental problem: how to reconcile the need to provide sufficiently powerful motive power capable of hauling (ever increasing) tonnages over maximum gradients of 1 in 25 with a locomotive which could negotiate a minimum curve (on the 'mainline') of 38m radius. Whilst the early Hagans and Krauss 0–4–0WTs and 0–6–0WTs with their short wheelbases easily met the latter criterion, by the 1890s there was evident need for more powerful motive power. For the OSB, the solution lay in some form of articulation.

Locomotives of the OSB *continued*			
0–6–0WT (later KPEV T31)			
OSB		KPEV 1904	KPEV 1911
18	KrMü	418/1875	
19		419/1875	
20		420/1875	
21		421/1875	
22		422/1875	
23		423/1875	
24		618/1876	
25		619/1876	
26		620/1876	
27		621/1876	
28	Hag	60/1877	Kat 28	Kat 6
29		67/1877	Kat 29	
30	KrMü	623/1877		
31		624/1877		Kat 1
32	Hag	77/1878	Kat 32	Kat 2
33		78/1878	Kat 33	Kat 3
34	KrMü	625/1877		Kat 4
35		762/1879		Kat 7
36		819/1879		Kat 8
37		820/1879		Kat 5
38		892/1880		
39		893/1880		Kat 9

Four locos allocated 99 7401–4 in the 1925 DRB renumbering scheme, but never carried

Locomotives of the OSB *continued*			
0–6–0T (later KPEV T31¹)			
		KPEV 1911	DRB
40	KrMü	1100/1884	Kat 10
41		1101/1884	Kat 11
42		1102/1884	Kat 12
43		1486/1884	Kat 13
44		1487/1884	Kat 14
45		1488/1884	
46		1489/1884	Kat 15
47		1490/1884	
48		2013/1888	Kat 16
49		2014/1888	Kat 17
50		2015/1888	Kat 18
51		2016/1888	Kat 19
52		2251/1890	Kat 20
53		2252/1890	Kat 21
54		2366/1890	Kat 22
55		2367/1890	Kat 23
56		2368/1890	Kat 24
57		2512/1891	Kat 25
58		2513/1891	Kat 26
47"		3292/1893	Kat 27
59		3375/1896	Kat 28
60		3376/1896	Kat 29	99 7411
61		3377/1896	Kat 30	(99 7412)
62		3678/1897	Kat 31
63		3679/1897	Kat 32
64		3680/1897	Kat 33
65		4153/1899	Kat 34
66		4154/1899	Kat 35	(99 7413)
67		4155/1899	Kat 36

Seven (or 10) T31¹ were acquired by the PKP but full details are not available

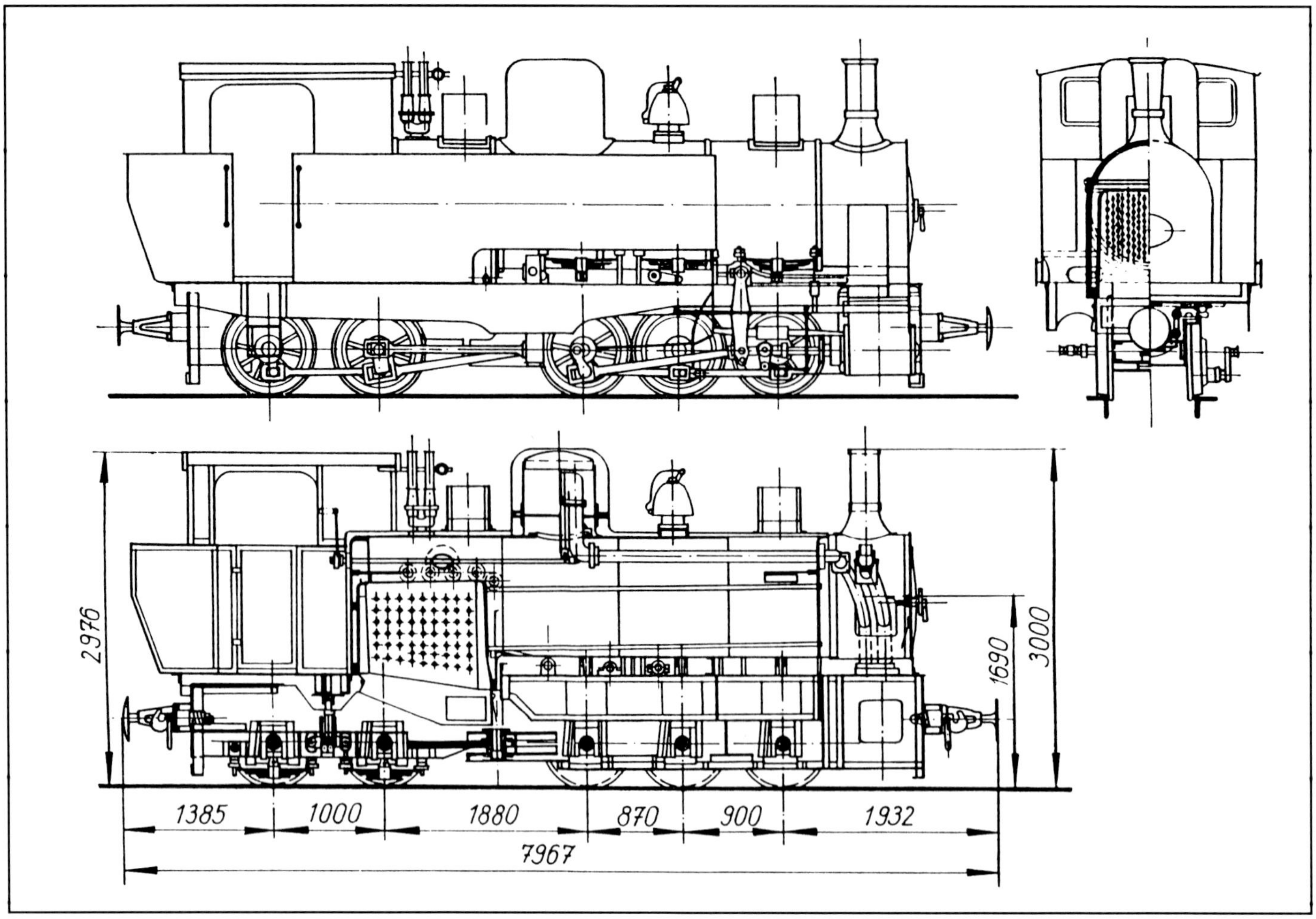

Its first attempt in this direction was, however, not conspicuously successful. Four articulated 0–10–0Ts were delivered by Hagans in 1896 (two) and 1901 (two). The first three axles were coupled in a conventional manner; the rear pair were also driven, being connected to the front set by a long coupling rod fitted with universal joints. This arrangement did not prove satisfactory in practice and the articulated coupling rods to the rear axles were soon removed. The four locos now ran as 0–6–4Ts, albeit rather ungainly ones as the wheels of the rear bogie were the same diameter as the coupled driving wheels. They were classified T36 by the KPEV in 1904.

Though still in existence, the locos did not feature on an OSB loco list compiled in 1918. The fate of T36.101 is unknown, but T36.102/3 were sold in 1923 to the Rhein-Sieg-Eisenbahn. T36.104 had the most eventful career and survived the longest. After World War I it was sold to the Rosenberger Kreisbahn and regauged to 750mm. When this line was rebuilt to standard gauge in 1928, the loco was acquired by the sugar factory at Stavenhagen. By 1945 it had reached the island of Rügen, though it never received a number from the privately owned Rügensche Kleinbahnen. The short-lived PLB did, however, allocate it, together with the other RüKB locos, a number – 265 – though this was never carried. When all these lines were absorbed into the DR in 1949, it became 99 4621. It remained on Rügen and was finally withdrawn in 1966.

The OSB's first attempt at articulation was this unusual Hagans Patent 0–10–0T. In service unsatisfactory, the rear coupling rods were soon removed and the locos ran as 0–6–4Ts. No. 8 (Hagans 441/1901) was photographed with the false worksplate attached: no. 443!
Collection: Uwe Bergmann

Class T37 (0–8–0T)

Clearly an alternative to the T36 had to be found and with its next essay into articulation the OSB was more successful. After several attempts, a design by O&K was settled upon. The specifications received by O&K for the proposed new locomotive speak volumes about the conditions faced by the OSB: 'Gauge 785mm, weight in service 28t, maximum axle loading 3.5t. The loco must be able to easily negotiate curves of 35m radius (opened out by 6mm) in both directions.'

Though essentially an O&K design, the first two were built by Hartmann in 1902 and differed in appearance from the later O&K and Hagans locos. They were outside frame 0–8–0Ts with Klien-Lindner axles on the outer two axles. The two inner axles were spaced at only 1,600mm, compared with the 1,800mm of the T31. With an enlarged boiler, an additional coupled axle and the enhanced ability to go round sharp curves afforded by the Klien-Lindner system, the OSB at last had a loco which could move heavy tonnages around its network in Upper Silesia; as a report of 1912 confirms: 'The 0–8–0T narrow gauge locos have fulfilled all our expectations of them.'

The two Hartmann locos were the last new locos of the Pringsheim regime on the OSB. After the KPEV assumed responsibility for operating the line in 1904, it classified the 0–8–0Ts T37. Between then and 1912, a further 18 were ordered from O&K and Hagans (two). All survived World War I.

Eight were taken into the stock of the DRB in 1922, with the final one being withdrawn in 1933. Ten went to the PKP, of which six were still in service in 1939 at the beginning of the German occupation. All had been withdrawn, however, before the 1942 renumbering.

Locomotives of the OSB *continued*

0–6–4T (later KPEV T36)

OSB		KPEV	Rhein-Sieg Eisenbahn	Rosenberger Krb	PLB	DR
5"	Hag 347/1896	T36.101	—	—	—	—
6"		348/1896	102	102	—	—
7"		440/1901	103	103	—	—
8"		441/1901	104	—	5	265	99 4621

The first really successful design for the OSB was a batch of 20 0–8–0Ts with Klien-Lindner axles, KPEV class T37. The first two, nos 9 and 10, were Hartmann products of 1902.
Collection: Uwe Bergmann

The 18 T37s built by O&K and Hagans differed in appearance from the Hartmann locos. 99 401 (O&K 1431/1904) was one of eight locos taken into DRB stock in 1922.
Collection: Uwe Bergmann

Locomotives of the OSB *continued*

0–8–0T (Klien Lindner) KPEV T37

KPEV 1904	KPEV 1911			DRB	PKP–A
Kat 9"	Kat 111	Hart	2775/1902	wd 1922 and sold	
10"	112		2776/1902	wd 1922 and sold	
11"	113	O&K	1430/1904	—	T37–2520
12"	114		1431/1904	99 401	—
13"	115		1432/1905	—	T37–2521
14"	116		1433/1905	99 402	—
15"	117		1474/1905	—	T37–2522
16"	118		1475/1905	—	T37–2523
17"	119		2146/1907	99 403	—
18"	120		2147/1907	—	T37–2524
19"	121		2148/1907	99 404	—
20"	122		2149/1907	99 405	—
21"	123	Hag	604/1909	—	T37–2525
22"	124		605/1909	99 406	—
23"	125	O&K	4343/1910	—	T37–2526
24"	126		4344/1910	—	T37–2527
—	127		5066/1912	—	T37–2528
—	128		5067/1912	99 407	—
—	129		5068/1912	99 408	—
—	130		5069/1912	—	T37–2529

Class T38 (0–8–0T)

Though the T37 represented a great improvement over all that had gone before, by 1914, as a result of the boom in traffic under the enthusiastic leadership of Geheimrat Stambke and the rapid technical developments (notably superheat) in the first decade of the 20th century, it too was being considered inadequate. In that year, O&K developed a more powerful 0–8–0T, which whilst based on the T37, differed from it in several important respects. The T38 was the first design on the OSB to employ superheat (Schmidt type). Between 1915 and 1919, a total of 26 were built.

Other changes to the T38 reflected the design developments being made in the years prior to 1914. Whereas the T37 had been a fully conventional, almost handsome, 0–8–0T, the T38 was both angular and functional looking. The boiler was pitched higher and the side tanks were smaller, though additional water was carried in a well tank. The most characteristic feature of the T38 was, however, the sharply angled cylinders, located high on the frames. This was due to the limited loading gauge of the OSB, which forced the designers to keep the cylinders in as tight as possible to the locomotive. As a consequence, the driving rod was unusually placed inside the coupling rods. The need to keep the overall width of the locomotive to a minimum also meant that the valve gear had no normal eccentrics. Instead the right hand driving crank served as the eccentric for the left hand sleeve drive and vice-versa. The motion was transferred by the crosshead and reduced by a lever mechanism.

With its raised, sharply angled cylinders, the T38 was the ugly duckling amongst the locos of the Upper Silesian NG. No. 213, shown here in KPEV livery, was finally withdrawn by the PKP in the 1950s.
Collection: Uwe Bergmann

Looking like a 2–6–2T, T39 no. 99 435 (O&K 8840/1920) was in fact an 0–10–0T fitted with Luttermöller axles. The T39s were to form the basis of all subsequent designs for the OSB.
Collection: Uwe Bergmann

Locomotives of the OSB *continued*

0–8–0T KPEV T38

KPEV			DRB/22	PKP–A	DRB/42	PKP–B/47	PKP–B/61	Kopalnia Wieczorek
Kat 211	O&K	7161/1915	—	T38–2540	99 401"	—		
212		7162/1915	—	T38–2541	99 402"	Tx6–2351		
213		7163/1915	—	T38–2542	99 403"	Tx6–2352		
214		7164/1915	—	T38–2543	99 404"	Tx6–2353		8
215		7165/1915	99 411	—	—	—		
216		7166/1515	99 412	—	—	—		
217		8151/1916	—	T38–2544	99 405"	Tx6–2354		
218		8152/1916	99 413	—	—	—		
219		8153/1917	—	T38–2545	99 406"	Tx6–2355		
220		8154/1917	—	T38–2546	99 407"	Tx6–2356		
221		8155/1917	—	T38–2547	99 408"	Tx6–2357	Tx9–2360	
222		8156/1917	—	T38–2548	99 409	Tx6–2358		
223		8157/1917	—	T38–2549	99 410	Tx6–2359		
224		8158/1917	99 414	—	—	—		
225		8223/1917	99 415	—	—	—		
226		8224/1917	99 416	—	—	—		
227		8225/1917	99 417	—	—	—		
228		8226/1917	—	T38–2550	99 411"	Tx6–2360	Tx9–2361	
229		8227/1917	—	T38–2551	99 412"	Tx6–2361	Tx9–2362	
230		8406/1918	99 418	—	—	—		
231		8407/1918	—	T38–2552	99 413"	Tx6–2362		
232		8408/1918	—	T38–2553	99 419"	Tx6–2364		
233		8409/1918	99 419	—	—	—		
234		8410/1918	99 420	—	—	—		
235		8731/1919	—	T38–2554	99 420"	—		7
236		8732/1919	—	T38 2555	99 421"	Tx6–2365		
237		8733/1919	99 421	—	—	—		

The Klien-Lindner system was chosen once again, but in a modified form. In comparison with the T37, the middle two axles were rigid in the frames. There was no connection between the middle and outer axles, but instead the end axles were formed as a Bissel truck. Like the T37, the T38 had outside frames.

In 1922, 11 T38s went to the DRB and 15 to the PKP. On the German side, six had been withdrawn by 1939, but all the Polish locos remained in service to be taken over by the DRB and renumbered in 1942, often assuming the numbers of withdrawn DRB T38s. Most of these survived the war and were taken into PKP stock in 1945 (as class Tx6, later Tx9). Withdrawal took place in the 1950s following the introduction of the more powerful and 'modern' Tw47 and Tw53.

Class T39 (0–10–0T)

The final KPEV locomotive development for the OSB was to form the basis of all subsequent designs for this railway. With the end of World War I, the need for yet more powerful locomotives could no longer be ignored. In 1919–20 O&K built seven superheated 0–10–0Ts fitted with Luttermöller axles on the two outermost axles giving the loco the superficial appearance of a 2–6–2T.

Locomotives of the OSB *continued*

0–10–0T PEV T39

PEV			DRB/22	PKP–A	DRB/42	PKP–B/47	PKP–B/61
Kat 251	O&K	8734/1919	99 431	—	—	—	—
252		8735/1919	—	T39–2560	99 436	—	—
253		8836/1920	—	T39–2561	99 437	—	—
254		8837/1920	99 432	—	—	Tw3–2438	Tw9–2470
255		8838/1920	99 433	—	—	Tw3–2437	Tw9–2469
256		8839/1920	99 434	—	—	—	—
257		8840/1920	99 435	—	—	—	—

So successful were the Prussian built T39s that the DRB had a further five constructed in 1923–24. Two of these worked on the PKP into the 1960s.
Collection: Uwe Bergmann

Locomotives of the OSB *continued*

0–10–0T T39 for DRB

DRB			PKP–B/47	PKP–B/61
99 441	O&K	10601/1923	Tw3–2434	Tw9–2467
99 442		10602/1923	—	—
99 443		10603/1924	—	—
99 444		10991/1925	—	—
99 445		10992/1925	Tw3–2435	Tw9–2468
99 446		10993/1925	Tw3–2436	—

The problem of providing cylinders sufficiently large for a locomotive of this size within the restricted loading gauge of the OSB was solved by raising the cylinder block and sloping it. A further potential difficulty of adequate coupling rod big ends on driving wheels of such small diameter (820mm) was also avoided by the use of the Luttermöller system, as tractive effort was applied to the driving wheels not only conventionally through the coupling rods, but also via the gears between the frames. With a rather low boiler centre (only two metres above rail level), the T39s looked somewhat compact and squat.

The first two appeared in 1919, followed by the remainder in 1920. When the OSB was divided in 1922, two T39s were acquired by the PKP. A further six locos to a similar design were delivered to the RBD Oppeln of the DRB by O&K between 1923 and 1925. These differed from the original batch in having wheels of 850mm diameter and axle loadings increased from eight to nine tonnes. Two of the 1919 and two of the 1923 series survived World War II to be absorbed into the reconstituted PKP as class Tw3 (later Tw9).

The PKP between the wars

Like the DRB, the PKP also looked to the T39 for its future requirements on its part of the OSB. Thus in 1923 Schwartzkopff delivered to the Poles as war reparations five 0–10–0Ts based very closely on the T39 and classified T40. These differed in one fundamental aspect which was to cause the Poles great problems: they were not fitted with Luttermöller axles.

The order for these locos was placed by the Ministry of Transport in Warsaw. Under the direction of the Polish engineer, Professor Czeczott, an attempt was made to achieve a loco with a flexible wheelbase without resorting to the (admittedly) rather complicated Luttermöller system. (Conjecture only, but perhaps the Poles were also unwilling to pay O&K for the licence rights for the Luttermöller patent.)

Whatever the reason, Czeczott specified a conventional loco with axle sideplay as follows: axle 1 – 0mm; 2 – 26mm; 3 – 0mm; 4 & 5 – 26mm. The third axle was flangeless. The rear two axles were connected by a double-flanged lever which was attached to

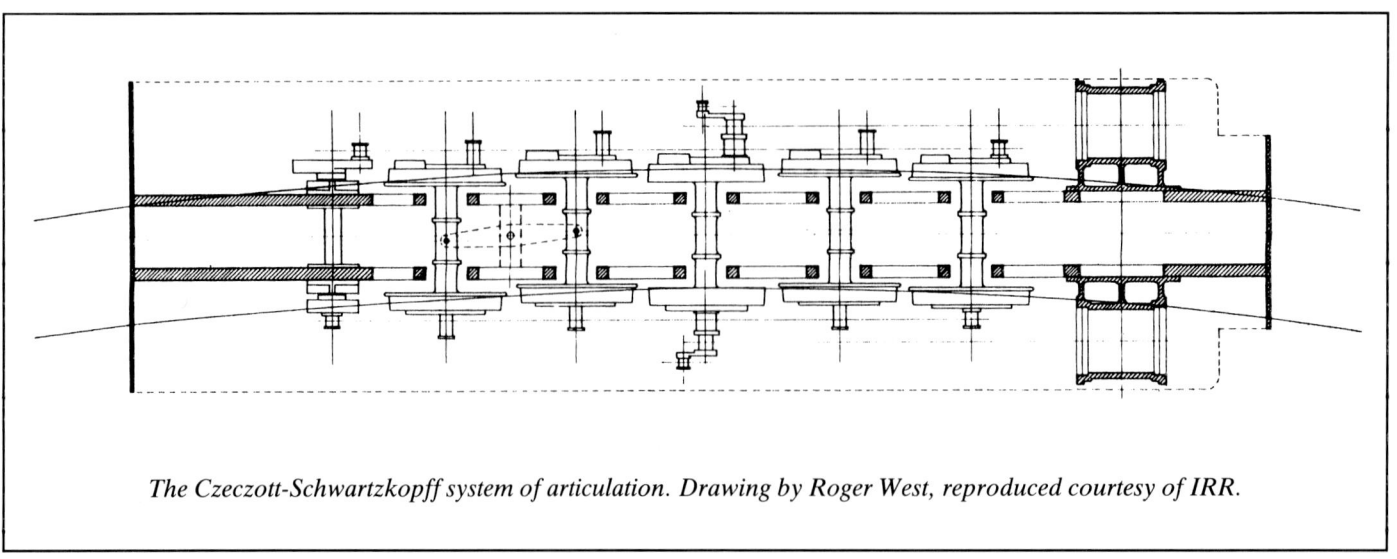

The Czeczott-Schwartzkopff system of articulation. Drawing by Roger West, reproduced courtesy of IRR.

The lay axle of the Czeczott system proved troublesome and was abandoned in the batch of six 0–10–0Ts built by Chrzanów in 1929. Tw29–2484, Bytom, May 1974.
Klaus Kieper

the transverse bar of the frames and which could revolve. Located behind the fifth axle there was a lay shaft with an outer crank to provide parallel guidance of the coupling rod to the loco axle to prevent bending or distortion of the coupling rods. In practice, however, it turned out that the lay shaft, as a consequence of movement of the fifth axle, was overloaded and frequently ran hot, even leading to total failure of the axleboxes. Nevertheless, Schwartzkopff built further locos based on Czeczott's principles; some of these are still hard at work in sugar mills in Java.

In 1928, Chrzanów received an order for another six 0–10–0Ts, but in light of the experience with the Berlin locos, the rear lay shaft was dispensed with and the coupled axles were given the following sideplay: axle 1 – 0mm; 2 – 15mm; 3 – 0mm (flangeless); 4 – 0mm; 5 – 26mm. This revised arrangement proved successful; otherwise there were few differences from the original 1919 O&K design for the KPEV. These locos and the (now modified?) BMAG 0–10–0Ts, rated at 400HP, formed the backbone of the PKP fleet on the OSB between the wars.

All the BMAG locos and five of the Chrzanów 0–10–0Ts were renumbered by the DRB in 1942 and all became PKP locos again in 1945 (classes Tw4, later Tw9, and Tw29). With the increasing dieselisation of the OSB in the 1960s and 1970s, the PKP tried to find further uses for the displaced steam locos; rebuilding and/or regauging them was an obvious solution and one such effort was to regauge Tw9–2464 (ex T40–2603) to 750mm gauge in 1971. It was thereupon renumbered Tw9–1451. Subsequently it was rebuilt to an 0–10–0 and became Pw9–1971.

After 1945 – the final phase

In 1946–47, Poland acquired through UNRRA 30(?) superheated narrow gauge 0–8–0s which had been built by Davenport (Iowa). Eight of these were converted to 785mm gauge and ran until the early 1970s on the OSB; the remainder were used on the 750mm lines of the PKP and, it is assumed, on 750/785mm gauge industrial lines. They were classified type Pxu, with the 'u' indicating the locos had come from UNRRA.

Whilst these American 0–8–0s were undoubtedly useful and a welcome addition to the motive power fleet in the immediate postwar period, they were not really suited to the special requirements of the OSB. This and the disastrous consequences of the growing political divide in Europe meant that the Poles were soon compelled to consider providing their own new locos for the OSB. As so often after World War II, they turned to an existing design rather than develop a new one. And such was the case with the 0–10–0Ts constructed by Chrzanów for the OSB after 1947. The boiler heating surface was increased by approximately 6m^3. The external appearance was altered by slightly reducing the size of the watertanks and coal bunker. But essentially the loco was little more than a clone of the 1919 O&K design minus the Luttermöller axles. Two batches of ten each were built for the PKP which designated them Tw47 and Tw53, reflecting their year of construction or that in which they were ordered.

Locomotives of the OSB *continued*
Locos acquired by PKP 1919–39

0–10–0T Reparations

PKP–A		DRB/42	PKP–B/47	PKP–B/61
T40–2600	BMAG 8359/1923	99 451	Tw4–2461	Tw9–2461
T40–2601	8360/1923	99 452	Tw4–2462	Tw9–2462
T40–2602	8361/1923	99 453	Tw4–2463	Tw9–2463
T40–2603	8362/1923	99 454	Tw4–2464	Tw9–2464
T40–2604	8363/1923	99 455	Tw4–2465	Tw9–2465

1971 Tw9–2464 to Tw9–1451" (regauged to 750mm) to Tw9–2451 (regauged to 785mm) to Pw9–1971 (rebuilt to 0–10–0 and regauged to 750mm)

0–10–0T Chrzanów

PKP–A		DRB/42	PKP–B/47
T40–2610	Chrz 313/1929	99 456	Tw29–2481
T40–2611	314/1929	99 457	Tw29–2482
T40–2612	315/1929	99 458	Tw29–2483
T40–2613	409/1929	99 459	Tw29–2484
T40–2614	410/1929	99 460	Tw29–2485
T40–2615	465/1929	—	—

At least nine of these typically American ng 0–8–0s, supplied by Davenport to UNRRA in 1945–46, worked on the PKP 785mm gauge lines in Upper Silesia as class Pxu.
Collection: Robert Koch

Locomotives of the OSB *continued*
Locos acquired by PKP after 1945

0–8–0 UNRRA

Pxu–2651	Dav	2859/1945	→ Pxu–1777 – 1867 – 2658	785mm → 750mm
2652		2860/1946	1868	
2653		2861/1946	1870	
2654		2862/1946	—	
2655		2870/1946	ex Pxu–1775 – 1865	750mm → 785mm
2656″		2871/1946	1776 – 1866	
2657		2853/1945	1773 – 1863	
2658		2859/1945	—	
2659″		2877/1946	1771 – 1861	

0–10–0T Tw47/53

Tw47–2551–2555   Chrz   1671–1675/1947
    2556–2560   Chrz   1676–1680/1948

Tw47–2551 1958 to industry; replaced at later date by Chrz 1919/1949 (from industry) becoming Tw47–2551″

Tw53–2561	Chrz	3990/1954
2562		3994/1954
2563		2645/1954
2564		2646/1954
2565		2647/1954
2566		2648/1954
2567		2649/1954
2568		2450/1954
2569		2451/1954
2570		2452/1954

1971 Tw53–2564 to Pw53–1980 (rebuilt to 0–10–0 and regauged to 750mm)

0–8–0 Px48

Px48–2701	Chrz	3230/1954	to Px48–1927 (750mm)
2702		3240/1953	1926
2703		2252/1952	1925

40

The UNRRA class Pxu.

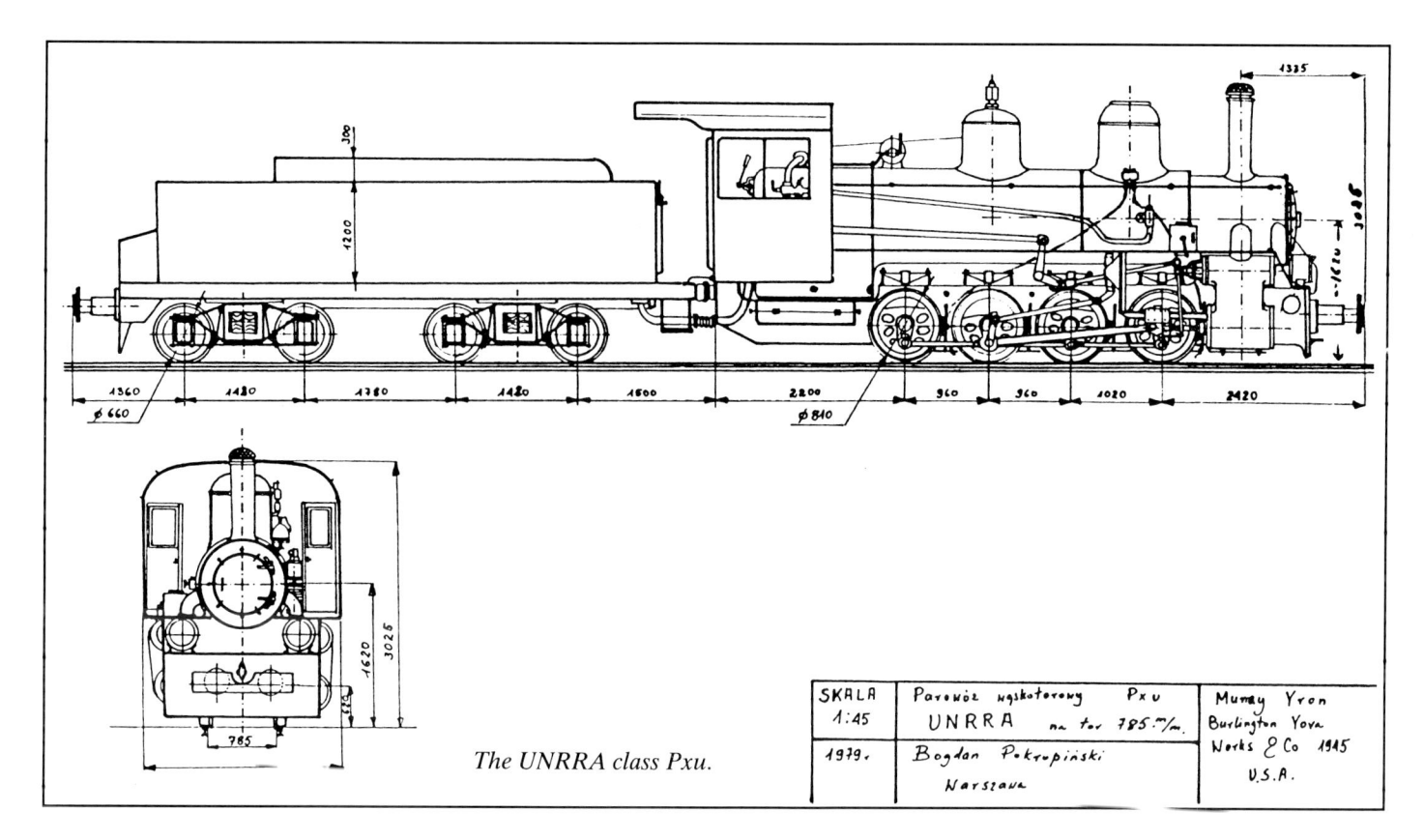

Between 1952 and 1955, three Px48 0–8–0s were supplied to the PKP for use on its 785mm lines in Upper Silesia. With ever encroaching dieselisation, they were rebuilt to 750mm in 1965–68 and became Px48–1925–7. Px48–1925 and 1927 were among the last active Px48s on the PKP, still working out of Gniezno MPD in 1993. Tw53–2564 was similarly regauged to 750mm in 1971 and fitted with a tender. It was renumbered to Pw53–1980 and is now preserved in the museum at Sochaczew.

During the 1970s, the number of steam locomotives active on the OSB steadily declined as more and more Romanian built diesels (type Lxd 2) became available. By the beginning of the 1980s, the PKP still had about 10 serviceable Tw47/53 on its books; in practice, however, only two were being used on a regular basis, as shunters at Bytom and Zabrze. The final two, Tw53–2561 and 2566, were officially withdrawn in 1988, but had done little, if any, work in the years prior to this.

Eighteen(?) locos of the Tw47/53 design were constructed by Chrzanów in the 1950s for various industrial enterprises linked to the OSB. One of these (Tw53–13953) worked at Kościuszko Steel Works at Chorzów into the 1990s. Its final day of operation is reported to have been 21 June 1991, which marked both the end of steam on the 785mm system in Upper Silesia and the unique series of locos built for it.

On 21 June 1991 Huta Kościuszko at Chorzów was the venue for the final day of steam operations on the Upper Silesian NG, with this baleful duty falling to Tw53–13953; 13953 is probably the boiler number.
Andrzej Cichowicz

THE KOLOMNA 750mm GAUGE 0-8-0s AND THEIR YEARS IN ESTONIA

Peeter Klaus

An unidentified 0–8–0 on a bridge testing train at Kariste; these Kolomna built locos worked in Estonia for over 60 years.
Collection: Peeter Klaus

Towards the end of the nineteenth century, many new 750mm gauge lines were constructed in Russia. Some of these developed into quite extensive systems with heavy goods traffic. Motive power was initially a variety of small tank locos, ranging from 0–4–0Ts to 0–8–0Ts. These were partly built in Russia itself, but for the greater part by different manufacturers in Europe. Whilst these tanks were adequate for short local lines, on the larger systems they were underpowered and not economical in service.

Many of these lines were operated by the 'Première Société Russe des Chemins de fer à voie étroite' (or *Perwoje Obstchestwo*), which had been founded in St Petersburg in 1892 by engineer B. Jalovetsky. The 'First Company' expanded rapidly in the 1890s and was divided into three divisions: Ukraine (559km); Lithuania (272km) and Estonia (335km).

To meet the growing need for more powerful narrow gauge locomotives, the Kolomna locomotive works designed in 1895 an 0–8–0, designated type 60. This was the first tender loco built for 750mm gauge in Russia and the precursor of a whole family of narrow gauge 0–8–0s built by Kolomna over the next 50 years. Altogether 16 locos of type 60 were constructed and supplied to the 'First Company'.

| P.201–204 | Kolomna | /1895 |
| P.205–216 | | /1896 |

These locos were allocated to the Estonian and Lithuanian divisions of the 'First Company'. In 1916, the Lithuanian locos were evacuated and sent to the other two divisions.

At the beginning of 1897, Kolomna started to build a modified version of the 60. In Russian and Soviet literature, these locos are often classified as type 63, but in reality were an intermediate design. The boiler and tender of the 60 were retained, whilst the frames and valve gear were those of type 63, which was to be introduced the following year. A total of 32 locos were built to this transitional design. All were supplied to the 'First Company' for use on its southern division, in Ukraine.

The early locos on Russian ng lines were small and frequently underpowered. A.3, built by Cockerill in 1893, worked on the Ryazan–Vladimir Railway near Moscow.
Collection: Peeter Klaus

Type 60/63 T.241 Kolomna 2096/97 → E.V.R. D.61

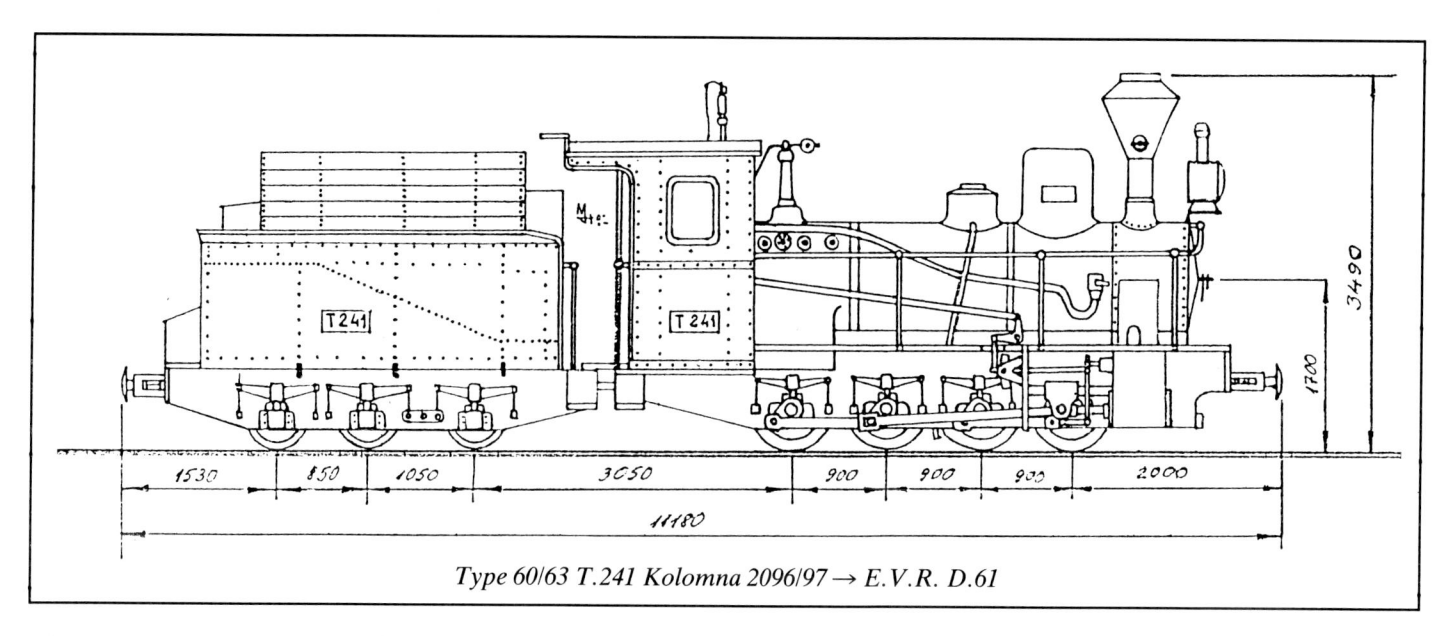

Kolomna's first ng tender loco was the class 60. P.203 belonged to the initial 1895 batch. In 1927 it became no. E.70 of the Estonian State Railways.   Collection: Peeter Klaus

Class 63 was a handsome 0–8–0. K.292 (works number 2406/1899) was one of 53 built by Kolomna between 1898 and 1903 for the 'First Company'.

Collection: Keith Chester

Type 60 P.203 → E.V.R. E.70

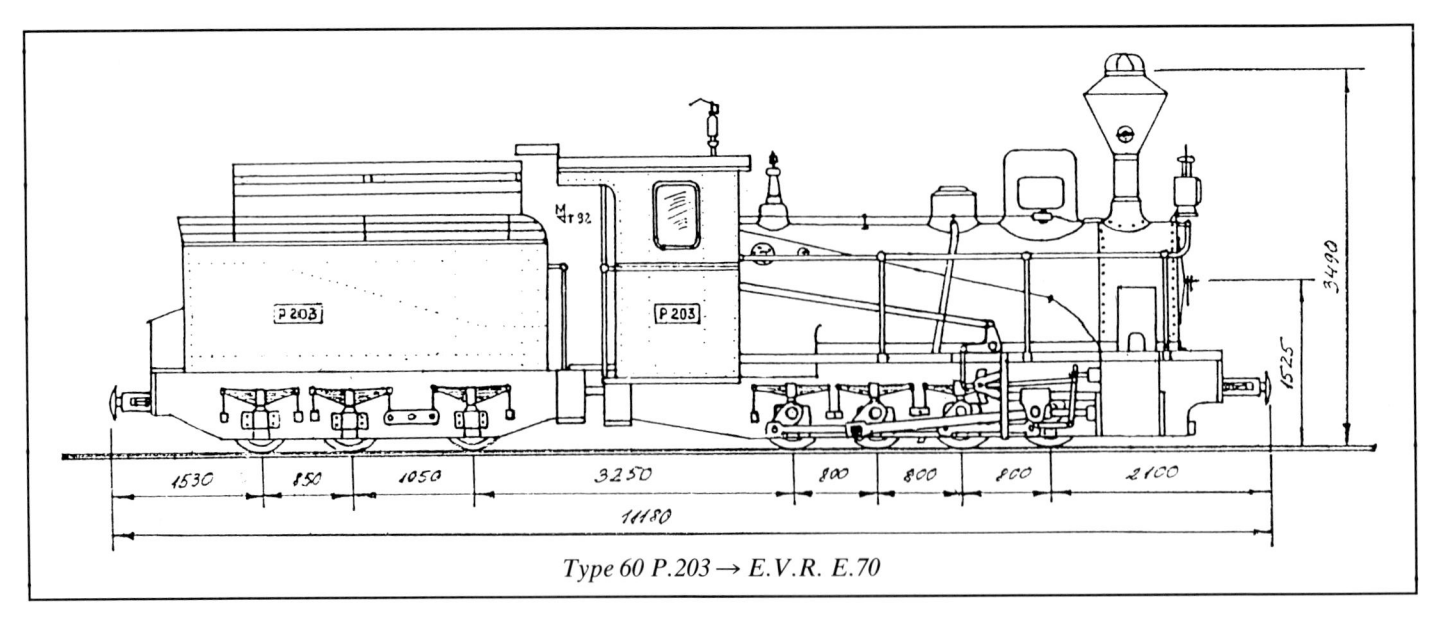

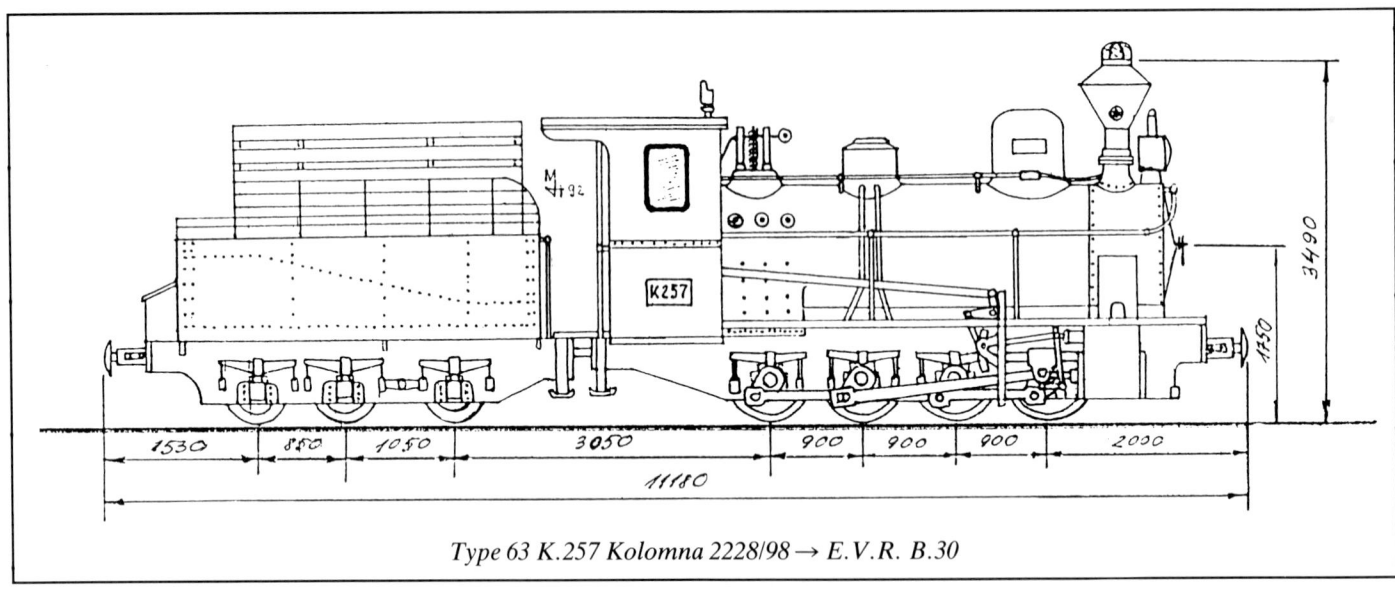

Type 63 K.257 Kolomna 2228/98 → E.V.R. B.30

21 class 63s were taken into the stock of the E.V.R. and renumbered in 1927. B.28, ex K.295, was photographed at Tallinn–Väike in 1928.
Collection: Peeter Klaus

T.217–236	Kolomna	2023–2042/1897
T.237–246		2092–2101/1897
T.247–248		2226–2227/1898

The first locos to the full-blown 63 design were produced in 1898. Between then and 1902, a total of 53 were delivered to the 'First Company', which numbered them K.249–302. In the same period, 13 were constructed for the 'Moscow Company of Secondary Lines'.

K.1–3	Kolomna	/1900
K.4–7		/1901
K.8–13		/1902

Two of these 0–8–0Ts were supplied new to the Moscow District Railways by Malt'sevskii in 1898. Their small wheels and tanks can hardly have made them suitable for mainline work.
Collection: Peeter Klaus

The 'Moscow Company' (also referred to as 'Moscow District Railway') had been founded in Moscow on 26 March 1892 (old Russian calendar). This concern was somewhat less ambitious than the 'First Company'. It only ever operated two lines (Ryazan pristan–Tuma–Vladimir (208km) and Tula–Lihvin (111km)) and did not even start building its first one until December 1897 – five and a half years after the company had been invested.

Construction of the type 63 continued until 1912, but quantities and purchasers are unknown.

An oil-fired variant of the 63, type 87, was developed in 1903, with all six locos going to the 'Moscow Company', where they were numbered K.20–25.

Type 122 was a superheated version of the 63 fitted with a Schmidt superheater. Only one loco was built, K^P.31 (Kolomna 4049/1910); this was acquired by the 'Moscow Company'. (NB. P = *peregrety* = superheated.)

Yet another modification to the 63 was type 127. Again only one loco was built (Kolomna 41xx/1911), but this time equipped with Stumpf cylinders. After construction it was displayed at the Torino world exhibition in 1911 before being sold to the 'Moscow Company'.

The next narrow gauge 0–8–0 to emerge from the Kolomna works was the type 65. 14 were supplied to the 'Livländische Zufuhrbahn-Gesellschaft'* in 1900–01; here they were numbered Ak.1–14. This company was established in 1898 and in 1903 opened the 750mm gauge line Valk–Marienburg (Aluksne)–Alt Schwarenburg (Gulbene)–Stockmanshof (Plavinas), which totalled 210km; Gulbene–Plavinas was converted to 1,524mm in 1916.

---

* *Zufuhrbahn* may be best rendered as 'feeder' railway, but this belies the true character of many such lines. After 1880 the construction of private railways in Czarist Russia virtually came to a halt. This was to protect the monopoly of the state-owned lines, as well as control the opening of railways in strategically sensitive border areas (e.g. the Baltic States and Poland). The only opportunity for a private entrepreneur was to build a narrow gauge railway and dub it a *Zufuhrbahn,* even if many of them, like that at Wolmar, were full-scale ng systems.

K.31 was a superheated version of the class 63; classified as type 122, only one was ever constructed. It was sold to the 'Moscow Company'.
Collection: Keith Chester

Type 65 Ak.20

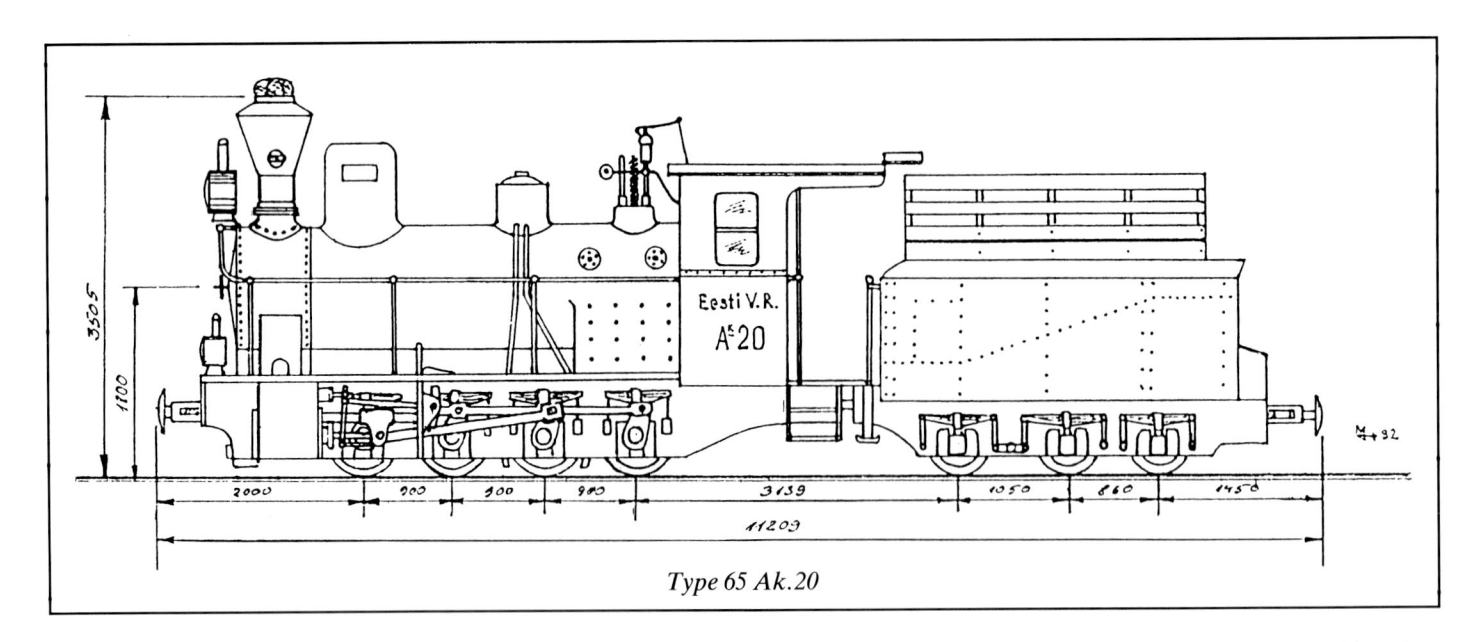

A further variant of the 63 was the 127, which was fitted with Stumpf cylinders. It was shown at the Torino world exhibition of 1911.
Collection: Peeter Klaus

This class 65 was originally constructed in 1900 for the 'Livländische Zufuhrbahn-Gesellschaft as its no. Ak.13; the E.V.R renumbered it A.13 in 1927. Valga, Estonia.
Collection: Peeter Klaus

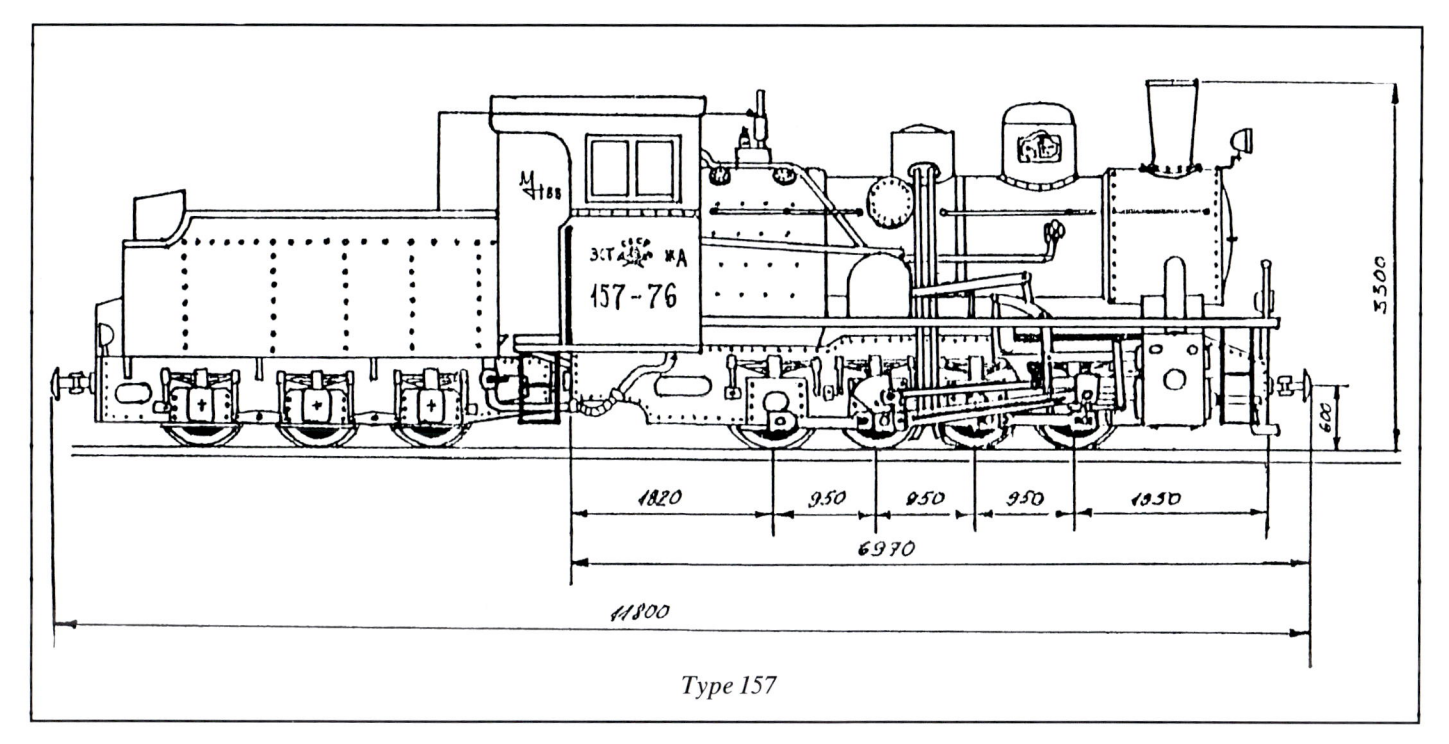

Type 157

The 'First Company' later took delivery of a further seven 65s.

K.303–307	Kolomna	3909–3913/1908
K.308		4125/1912
K.309		4159/1912

Five 65s were also built for the 113km 'Wolmarer Zufuhrbahn' in north-west Latvia, which was constructed in 1911–12.

A.1–3	Kolomna	4099–4101/1911
A.4–5		4123–4124/1911

A.4 and A.5 were lost as a result of World War I, but the other three were taken over by the LVD and renumbered Pp–751–753. Between 1924 and 1940, they regained their former numbers (A.1–3) and finally in 1940 reverted again to Pp–751–753!

The 65 was evidently successful in operation, as in 1916 it was chosen as a standard type for the Russian army and classified as type O. Construction for the military ceased in 1919, but production of the 65s continued until c. 1926. The peacetime locos were designated type K and were used principally on industrial railways in the USSR. A total of about 140–150 type 65 are estimated to have been constructed. They were widely distributed all over the Soviet Union.

When built none of the Kolomna 750mm gauge 0–8–0s described above had any brakes on the locos and had to make do with a handbrake on the tender. It is believed that only after World War II were a few locos modernised and equipped with steam brakes on the loco. Some of those which survived into the 1950s to work on Pioneer Railways were subsequently fitted with air pumps and brakes.

Construction of the 65 seems to have ended in 1926, by which time both the Soviet Railways and industrial enterprises in the USSR were in urgent need of more modern and powerful locos. Kolomna, however, showed little imagination and merely updated the 65 and 122 classes to produce a new design – the 157 – which fortunately was to prove to be the most successful narrow gauge locomotive in the Soviet Union for the next 20 years.

Kolomna built 47 157s in 1928–29. The exact works numbers are unknown, but are somewhere in the range 56xx–57xx/1928–29. The first 17 had smaller boilers. All were fitted with steel Belpaire fireboxes and Schmidt superheaters. Unlike their predecessors, the 157s were from the very beginning equipped with steam brakes, with handbrakes on the tenders. It is possible that some that worked on the SŽD were fitted with air brakes.

Pp–752 (Kolo 4100/1911) had a chequered history. Originally A.2 on the 'Wolmarer Zufuhrbahn', it was renumbered Pp–752 when taken over by the Latvian Railways after World War I; numbered A.2 between 1924 and 1940, it finally became Pp–752 again in that year. It was photographed at Ruhja in June 1956.
Collection: Peeter Klaus

Kolomna developed the 157 as a replacement for the 65 in the late 1920s. It is widely regarded as one of the most successful ng types to have operated in either Russia or the USSR. Sh–30 was the first to be transferred to Estonia sometime during World War II.
Collection: Peeter Klaus

It wasn't, however, until 1933 that extensive trials of the 157 were conducted. These were held on the Chernoramensk peat railway, Balahna, near Nizhni-Novgorod (Gorki). On test, the 157 proved economical in operation, with a highly efficient boiler. It was also a remarkably free running loco, with a permitted maximum speed of 40kmh, which it easily exceeded on trial. This may be compared with the Gr, a similar 0–8–0 which was introduced almost 20 years later and which rolled badly above 35kmph.

In 1936–37, but possibly earlier in 1935, the 'Red Sormovo' (*Krasnoje Sormovo*) works near Gorki built about 200 157s; again it is impossible to provide any precise details on the works numbers. There were few differences between the Kolomna built 157s and those which emerged from the Sormovo works, save the latter made a greater use of welding.

There were, however, considerable variations in the numbering schemes applied to the 157s:

157–3470 (Sormovo 3470/1937) came to Estonia c. 1945. It is seen here at the head of a freight train sometime in the 1950s.
Collection: Peeter Klaus

(1) Iron and steelworks:
    157K (= Kolomna) and 157S (= Sormovo) plus the final two numbers of the works number.
(2) SŽD:
    (a) The locos of the former southern division (Ukraine) of the 'First Company' were classified Ш (Sh), plus a special ng numbering system, Sh–1–35(?).
    (b) Zabaikal ng system (Back–Baikal). All locomotives displayed the class number, plus the works number, e.g. 157–3468, 157–3470.
    (c) Alapajevsk ng system. 157K or 157S, plus the last two numbers of the works numbers, e.g. 157K–25 (Kolomna 5725/1928), 157S–31 (Sormovo 3431/1936).
    (d) Beloretzk ng system. 157K or 157S, plus local number, e.g. 157K–74 (Kolomna 5727/1928).
(3) Various short lines:
    The class number, plus local numbering scheme, e.g. 157–469 on the Chernoramensk peat railway.
(4) Kirovgrad Copper Kombinat Railway:
    Kp or Sp, plus a local number.
    (Kp = *Kolomenskii parowoz* = Kolomna steam loco
    Sp = *Sormovskii parowoz* = Sormovo steam loco).

The variations seem to have been both endless and endlessly confusing!

The 157s were well-liked locomotives and continued to be widely used on both the SŽD and industrial lines after 1945. Many survived the influx of the more modern 0–8–0s of types Gr and PT–4/VP–1 in the late 1940s and the 1950s. Most were laid aside in the period 1963–67 and in many cases outlasted the Grs and the PT–4s etc. The final one in service appears to have been 157K–73 (Kolomna 5724/1928), which shunted on the Beloretzk narrow gauge system till about 1976–78.

Almost contemporary with the 157 was the 159; its genesis is described on page 96. Built in large numbers by various works, it was, however, a Kolomna design, though probably one the factory would have cheerfully disowned. Lacking sufficient superheat, it was the least successful of all the 750mm 0–8–0s to have emerged from the Kolomna works. Widely used on industrial lines and by the Soviet military railways in World War II, most disappeared in the 1950s and early 1960s.

THE KOLOMNA 0–8–0s IN ESTONIA

Many of the 0–8–0s described above were initially allocated to lines in Estonia and were nationalised in 1918. Later, on 31 October 1923, they were officially absorbed into the Estonian State Railways (*Eesti Vabariigi Raudtee*); after the loss of independence in 1940 they were also supplemented by some 157s. Thus for many years, and particularly in the inter-war period, the Kolomna 0–8–0s were the mainstay of the EVR's narrow gauge lines.

Those on the Estonian division of the 'First Company' were all nationalised in 1920. At first they ran under their former numbers and it was only in 1927 that the EVR renumbered them.

In 1941, 34 ex EVR narrow gauge locos were evacuated to Russia, few of which ever returned to Estonia after 1945. By the autumn of 1944, about 25 former Estonian narrow gauge locos were stored at a large dump at Piukule in northern Latvia. Again only a few ever saw service again in Estonia; some remained in Latvia, where they were renumbered in the Pp series; others were transferred to Russia in 1947 for use on industrial and forestry railways. Those in the worst condition, the majority, were cut up, having been damaged beyond economic repair by the *Wehrmacht* in its retreat in 1944.

The war years hit the Estonian railways harshly; from a total of 95 steam locomotives in July 1941, only 39 were in stock in September 1944. This had risen by a mere seven to 46 in 1948 and 51 in 1950. After 1945 only the following Kolomna 0–8–0s were still left in Estonia: E.72; T.245; B.31; B35; B.49; A.11; K.1 and K.4. Except for A.11, withdrawal of all these locos was complete by 1960.

159–189 was allocated to the 750mm lines of Estonia in June 1945. Four years later it was photographed at Viljandi. Collection: Peeter Klaus

Class 63 no. K.294 (Kolo 2408/1899) heads a typical mixed train of the 1920s in Estonia. *Collection: Peeter Klaus*

Newly renumbered B.41 (Kolo 2366/1899) transports the frame for the viaduct at Reiu, c. 1927. *Collection: Peeter Klaus*

In 1922 an unidentified 63 leaves Mõisaküla with a train for Pärnu. *Collection: Peeter Klaus*

A 65 hauled passenger crosses the bridge at Mavesti on the Võhma–Viljandi line in central Estonia in the years between the wars.
Collection: Peeter Klaus

Kolomna Types 60, 60/63, 63 and 65 in Estonia

	Works No./Year	Orig. No.	1927 No.	Remarks
Type 60				
Kolomna	/1896	P.203	E.70	
	/1896	P.208	E.71	
	/1896	P.211	E.72	1952 to Moscow–Kursk, wd 1958
	/1896	P.212	E.73	
	/1897	P.214	E.74	
	/1897	P.215	E.75	To Latvia Pp–75, wd 1945
	/1897	P.216	E.76	1945 to Latvia, 1951 to Rostov paper mill
Type 60/63				
Kolomna	2039/1897	T.233	D.60	1930–41 at Sonda MPD
	2096/1897	T.241	D.61	1930–41 at Sonda MPD
	2100/1897	T.245	—	1945 to Estonia, ex Gaivoron, Ukraine, wd 1955
Type 63				
Kolomna	2228/1898	K.249	B.30	1945 to Latvia
	2236/1898	K.257	B.31	wd 1963–64
	2237/1898	K.258	B.32	1945 to October Railway, wd 1950, peat fired
	2248/1898	K.259	B.33	
	2249/189x	K.260	B.34	To Latvia, wd 1947
	2250/189x	K.261	B.35	wd 1960
	2251/189x	K.262	B.36	
	2252/189x	K.263	B.37	
	2257/189x	K.268	B.38	To South West Railway (Vinnitsa), wd 1957
	2308/1899	K.278	B.39	
	2357/1899	K.279	B.40	To Latvia, wd 1947
	2366/1899	K.288	B.41	To Latvia, wd 1947
	2403/1899	K.289	B.42	To Latvia, wd 1947
	2404/1899	K.290	B.43	To Latvia, Pp–743
	2405/1899	K.291	B.44	
	2406/1899	K.292	B.45	
	2407/1899	K.293	B.46	
	2408/1899	K.294	B.47	
	2439/1900	K.295	B.48	
	2440/1900	K.296	B.49	wd 1960
	2441/1900	K.297	B.50	1945 to Latvia, 1947 to South West Railway (Vinnitsa), wd 1957
Kolomna	/1900		K.1	1945 to Estonia, ex Moscow Company, wd 1961
	/1901		K.4	1945 to Estonia, ex Moscow Company, 1958 to Kalinin stone crushing plant
Type 65				
Kolomna	/1908	K.303	A.10	To Latvia, wd 1947
	3910/1908(?)	K.304	A.21	
	/1900	Ak.11	A.11	wd 1963–64
	/1900	Ak.12	A.12	
	/1900	Ak.13	A.13	
	/1900	Ak.14	A.14	
	/1900	Ak.15	A.15	
	/1900	Ak.16	A.16	
	/1900	Ak.17	A.17	
	/1900	Ak.18	A.18	
	/1900	Ak.19	A.19	
	/1901	Ak.20	A.20	

The changing of the guard at Türi: left, class 65 no. A.11 a year or so before its withdrawal; right, Tu2–094, a diesel electric BoBo, then new in service. July 1962.
Collection: Peeter Klaus

Following the Soviet occupation of Estonia in October 1940, the EVR was absorbed into the SŽD. It is believed that as early as the autumn of 1940, plans existed for the transfer of some 157s to Estonia to strengthen the rather ageing ex EVR fleet of locos. Because of the course of the war, these plans were not implemented and only one 157 (Sh–30) reached Estonia; it was in stock by 1 June 1941. (NB. This loco does not appear on a 1943 stock list for the Estonian railways and perhaps only reached Estonia after this date.) The drastic losses to the Estonian loco fleet during the war made the transfer of new locos to Estonia essential and after 1945 157s and 159s were sent from Russia. Yet even these relatively modern locos were to see but a few years in service in Estonia, before they in turn were replaced by the new postwar Gr and PT–4s.

Eight of the less than satisfactory 159 class were officially allocated to Estonia as of 1 June 1945. These were nos 159–57, 189, 232, 237, 249, 286, 294 and 649 (or possibly 643). They were used principally for shunting and on mixed and secondary trains on the Valga–Mõniste and Sonda–Mustvee branches. Unloved and unwanted all had disappeared from Estonia by 1954, mostly going to Byelorussia.

The first three 157s to arrive in Estonia after World War II were 157S–3388, 3468 and 3470 (Sormovo 1937, with running numbers repeating the works numbers) from the Zabaikal narrow gauge system. They were allocated to Tallinn–Väike, Pärnu and Mõisaküla MPDs and, unlike the 159s, used on mainline trains. The initial three were followed in the autumn of 1956 by five more from the South Ural narrow gauge railway; these were 157–5, 7, 14, 15 and 27 (Sormovo 1936, works numbers unknown). They spent less than a year in Estonia before being reallocated to Byelorussia in 1957. That same year 157S–3388, 3468 and 3470, together with Sh–30, were transferred to the Virgin Land narrow gauge railways in the northern provinces of Kazakhstan, thereby ending the service of these highly successful 0–8–0s in Estonia.

As elsewhere, the 159s found little favour in Estonia and all had been reallocated away by 1954.
Collection: Peeter Klaus

FORESTRY RAILWAYS IN JUGOSLAVIA

Keith Chester

One of the immediate consequences of the occupation of Bosnia-Hercegovina by the Austro-Hungarian Empire in 1878 was its opening up to commercial exploitation. At that time much of the province was thickly wooded, with probably a greater population of wolves than of people, and not surprisingly the timber industry was one of the first to establish itself.

Its development was much promoted by the roads and 760mm railways built initially by and for the Habsburg armies, but which later served civilian and commercial purposes. The provincial government in Sarajevo was eager to encourage economic growth: land was leased and, with labour cheap, numerous logging companies soon sprang up. Once the easily exploitable stands alongside the new roads and railways and the main river valleys had been cleared, it was necessary to look to the side valleys for timber, from where the logs were less easily removed.

In the last quarter of the nineteenth century, the forestry railway provided the solution and a large number were constructed, principally in Bosnia-Hercegovina, but also throughout what was to become Jugoslavia. These varied from short, animal-powered lines, intended to last but a season or two until the timber supply was exhausted, to virtual 'mainline' systems such as the 400km long Steinbeisbahn, which operated a large fleet of modern and powerful locomotives and even provided scheduled passenger services. Gauge was (almost) invariably 760mm, conforming to that of the BHStB.

The sheer variety of motive power was almost incredible – even as late as the 1960s. Some lines survived into the 1970s, using steam until the very end.

Not quite what it seems: the Steinbeisbahn was a forestry railway and 0–8–0T+T no. 36 (Maff 3786/1912) is not hauling a mixed, but shunting empty stock, which it will shortly reverse back into Jajce station. 8 July 1964.
Alfred Luft

Otto Steinbeis was an early and enthusiastic user of Mallet tanks and over the years employed 23 0–4–4–0Ts, 0–4–4–2Ts & 0–6–6–0Ts. No 10, photographed at Mliniště on 13 August 1959, was completed by O&K in 1904, works number 1289.
Alfred Luft

The largest loco to be found on most forestry railways in Europe was eight-coupled, but the Steinbeisbahn, ever the line of superlatives, operated eight 0–10–0Ts and three 0–10–0s. A gleaming no. 30 (O&K 10828/1924) is seen here at Šipovo on 24 August 1967. Alfred Luft

Parts of the Steinbeisbahn remained in service until the mid 1970s, latterly using redundant class 73 2–6–2s – once the greyhounds of the BHStB – on the lightly graded section between Prijedor and Sanica Donja. 73–019 (Bp 3287/1913) shunts a long train of timber wagons at Prijedor on 28 August 1969. Today the loco is preserved at Frojach in Austria. Werner Fritthum

'Kusače' was one of two 0–6–2Ts supplied by Krauss, München in 1901 to the company of Eissler & Ortlieb. After 1918 their operations were nationalised and 'Kusače' remained at work on the Zavidovići–Kusače forestry line. Sister loco 'Stupcanica' (KrMü 4378/1901) was later transferred to the forestry railway at Maglići. Zavidovići, 10 August 1959. Alfred Luft

Large numbers of the RIIIc type 0–6–0T were constructed for the Austrian army (kkHB) during World War I. After the war many were sold to industrial lines in Austria and Central Europe, where some survived in service until the late 1970s. 'Bosna' (KrLi 7498/1918) was photographed at Zavidovići on 10 August 1959. Alfred Luft

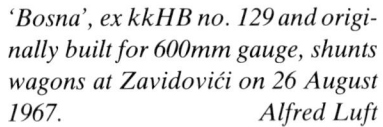

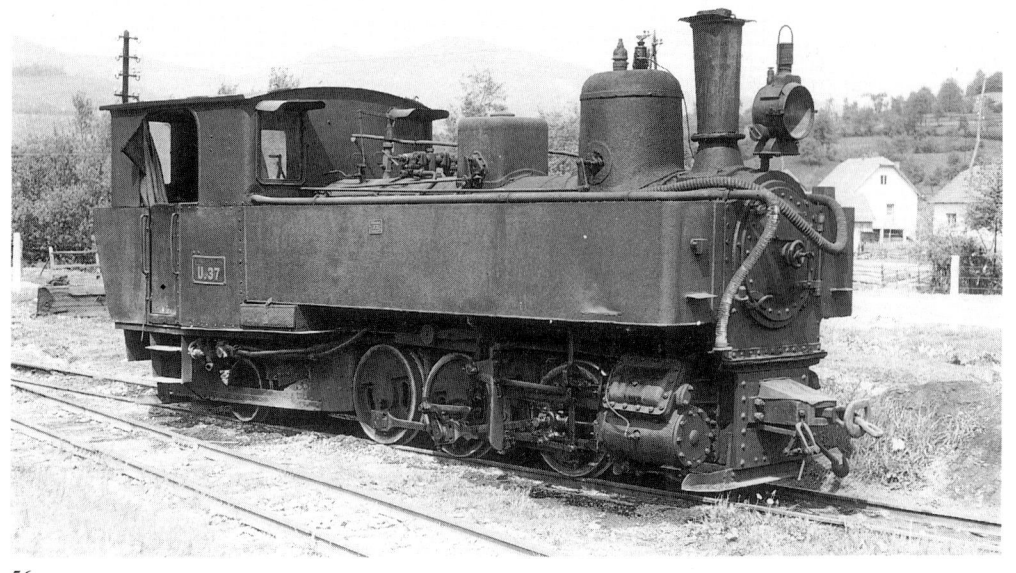

'Bosna', ex kkHB no. 129 and originally built for 600mm gauge, shunts wagons at Zavidovići on 26 August 1967. Alfred Luft

U.37 (WrN 4867/1908) was a much travelled loco. Delivered to the Triest–Parenzo railway in 1908, it was at Weiz in Styria in 1911. Six years later it was one of many locos transferred to the Steinbeisbahn for war work; in 1918 it came to the SHS and finally to Busovača, where it was still hard at work on 10 May 1971. Werner Fritthum

This 0–6–2T was manufactured by Krauss, Linz (works number 3838) for the Bosnische Holzverwertungs AG, Teslić, in 1898. The same year three identical 0–6–2Ts were supplied to the Gurkthalbahn in Austria as its class T (ÖBB class 198), but clearly no. 2 has been locally modified, receiving an enlarged bunker and sidetanks. Teslić, 26 August 1967.
Alfred Luft

Unlike no. 2, KrLi 4657/1901, another 'Gurkthalbahn' type, retained much of its original appearance; it had previously worked at Usora and Borja, but when noted on 7 July 1964 was at Ilijaš.
Alfred Luft

The Maglić forestry railway was probably the last classic forestry railway to operate in Jugoslavia – it even had an inclined plane. 0–8–0T no. 19–126 (Hens 19126/1923) was photographed on the upper section shunting a train of logs at Palež on 23 July 1970. The line closed three or four years later.
Werner Fritthum

Between 1905 and 1912 Krauss, Linz constructed eight of these light compound 0–8–0Ts for various industrial railways in the Monarchy and three for kkStB 760mm gauge lines in Galicia. The design was evidently satisfactory as the Salzkammergutbahn acquired a similar 0–8–0T in 1925. No. 5 (KrLi 5316/1908) was photographed on shed at Teslić on 11 August 1959.   Alfred Luft

The worksplate proclaims no. DD2 to be a Maffei loco, reputedly of 1906, but the Maffei list shows no 0–6–2Ts constructed that year, nor for many either side of it. Was DD2 a homemade product with a spare Maffei plate attached? Teslić, 26 August 1967.   Alfred Luft

Comparatively few Henschel locos worked on the forestry railways of Jugoslavia. 0–6–0T 'Vera' (Hens 20917/1927), ex Gostević, was captured on film shunting at Zavidovići sawmill on 26 August 1967.
Alfred Luft

Jung 0–8–0T (11928/1953) at work on the Srednje forestry railway in July 1961. The loco is ex Jahorina and one of a batch of eight supplied by Jung to the Servisza Industrija, Beograd in 1953.
Collection: Alfred Luft

The Zavidovići–Kusače forestry railway was owned by the province of Bosnia-Hercegovina and leased to Eissler & Ortlieb. In its 118.7km it had to climb more than 800 metres and required powerful locos for mainline work. 1394 was an 0–10–0T supplied by Krauss, Linz in 1925 and was photographed awaiting departure with a mixed at Olovo on 10 August 1959. The design was developed from 0–8–0Ts built in 1915 for the kkHB Grödnertalbahn in South Tirol.   *Alfred Luft*

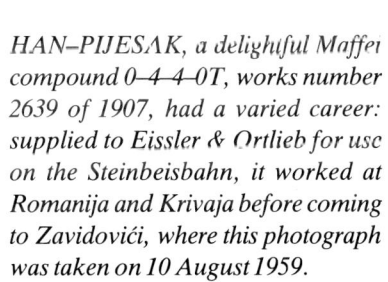

HAN–PIJESAK, a delightful Maffei compound 0–4–4–0T, works number 2639 of 1907, had a varied career: supplied to Eissler & Ortlieb for use on the Steinbeisbahn, it worked at Romanija and Krivaja before coming to Zavidovići, where this photograph was taken on 10 August 1959.
Alfred Luft

THE Px48 0–8–0s OF THE PKP

Keith Chester

When the Republic of Poland was declared in 1918 it lacked any domestic locomotive manufacturer. But within two years, with government prompting and financial guarantees, three – Cegielski, Chrzanów and Warszawa – had been established with the specific intention of reducing Poland's dependency on foreign locomotive manufacturers. Initially all three co-operated with foreign locomotive builders and leant heavily on their expertise.

By the late 1920s, however, sufficient experience and confidence had been gained and an attempt was made to break the stranglehold of the traditional suppliers (mainly German) to private and industrial railways in Poland. Thus at Chrzanów, a small department to serve this market was set up in 1926 and a number of new, Polish, narrow gauge and industrial designs were developed.

Among these were several narrow gauge 0–8–0Ts and here can be found the origins of the Px48. In 1927 Chrzanów received an order for two 750mm 0–8–0Ts (works numbers 177 & 184). These locos, classified W–3–A, were almost identical to the 1926 W–1–A type for 600mm, which was the first truly Polish narrow gauge design. Both the W–1–A and W–3–A were equipped with Heusinger valve gear and Friedmann injectors.

This works photo of the W–3–A is reproduced from a 1937 Chrzanów photo album.
Collection: Bogdan Pokropiński

The Wp29s were introduced in 1929 and 1930. They were the first modern, Polish narrow gauge design built in any number. An unidentified member of the class was photographed on the Kujawische system in 1936.
Collection: Bogdan Pokropiński

In 1929 the Transport Ministry placed an order for 21 750mm 0–8–0s with Warszawska Spółką Akcyjną Budowy Parowozów in Warsaw – the smallest locomotive manufacturer in Poland. These were designated 'Wilno' or Wp29, and were allocated to various districts of the PKP. Despite some initial problems with derailments, the Wp29s were smooth runners and popular locos with crews and maintenance staff alike. One loco, Wp29–3005 (War 156/1929), was built for 760mm gauge and sent to the Łupków–Cisna railway. It does not seem to have been particularly successful there, being perhaps somewhat underpowered compared with its kkStB predecessors; it is possible too that its longer wheelbase did not suit the numerous and rather sharp curves of this line. It has been suggested that when the loco received a general repair in 1936 the opportunity was taken to regauge it to 750mm and it was transferred to the DOKP Wilno. All trace of the loco is lost after 1939 and it may be safely assumed that it disappeared somewhere in the Soviet Union.

When Hitler and Stalin divided up Poland between them in 1939, 11 Wp29s fell to the DRB and were renumbered 99 2574–84 in 1942. These all survived the war and became Px29–1701–11 in the re-constituted PKP. The final loco was withdrawn in 1977 but fortunately two, Px29–1704 and 1708, have been preserved at the narrow gauge museum at Sochaczew near Warsaw. Px29–1704 was restored to working order in the mid 1980s but had to be withdrawn needing substantial boiler repairs in 1992. The loco was overhauled in the course of 1993 and was expected to return to service in 1994. A further four Px29s have been preserved at Hillerstorp in Sweden.

Of the 10 Wp29s that went to the USSR, six are known to have worked on various lines in the Baltic States and two in Ukraine. An official list, dated 13 January 1958, records nos Tch–153, 154 and 1732 as being allocated to the Byelorussian Railway, which suggests some reallocations. In the early 1950s, the class began to be replaced by more modern 0–8–0s of type 'Gr', built as war

Two Wp29s cautiously head a freight train over the viaduct at Lubraniec on the Kujawische system. c. 1936.
Collection: Bogdan Pokropiński

By the 1950s those Wp29s which had remained in the USSR were serving out their days on Pioneer Railways. Rp–771 (ex Wp29–458?) is seen here on the Kratovo Pioneer Railway near Moscow.
Collection: Peeter Klaus

reparations for the Soviet Union by LKM Babelsberg. However, a few of the Wp29s survived into the 1960s, working out their final years on that most socialist of institutions – the Pioneer Railway.

Technically, the Wp29 very closely followed the Chrzanów designs which had preceded it, particularly the W–3–A. By attaching a four-wheel bogie tender the range of operations was extended to up to 65kms. The application of superheat and improved firebox design meant that the performance of the 'Wilno' was markedly superior to that of the Chrzanów narrow gauge locos. On level track, the Wp29 could pull 300 tonnes at 25kmph. The minimum radius negotiable was 35m; to permit this, the fourth axle had a side play of 15mm and the wheels of the second axle a reduced profile. The Wp29 displayed many features typical of Polish design such as Heusinger valve gear and Friedmann lubricators. Braking was both manual and by Westinghouse air brake.

The Px29 formed the basis of the Px48 design. In 1943 K. Sielecki, an engineer at Chrzanów, discovered the technical data and drawings of the Wp29 amongst German files held at Kraków (Chrzanów had been taken over by Henschel during the period of the Nazi occupation) and was able to 'rescue' them for the Chrzanów archives. Poland had a desperate need for all types of motive power after World War II, not least narrow gauge. In most cases the Poles found it easier and quicker to modify and modernise an existing design, rather than produce an entirely new one. Thus out of the Px29 was the Px48 born. In appearance the Px48 was a more modern looking locomotive than the Px29 and offered the crews a more commodious and protected cab. Yet a close study of the principal dimensions reveals how fundamentally similar the two designs were.

The first 10 Px48s appeared in 1950 and between then and 1955, a further 94 were constructed by Chrzanów for the 750mm lines of the PKP. This coincided with moves by the PKP to introduce some degree of standardisation and modernisation to the 40 or so narrow gauge lines it had inherited in 1945. Together these totalled approximately 3,900km and were of varying gauges, ranging from 600 to 1,000mm. The motive power situation was equally

Tch–155 (ex Wp29–4585) working on an unknown Pioneer Railway.
Collection: Peeter Klaus

The re-formed PKP absorbed 11 Wp29s in 1945 and reclassified them Px29; withdrawal took place during the 1970s. Px29–1701 was photographed at Wresniec in 1970.
Bogdan Pokropiński

unpromising: the new PKP had some 500 narrow gauge locos on its books, but only 63 of these were less than 10 years old. Faced with this situation, the PKP took the opportunity of regauging many lines to 750mm and at the same time introducing modern and more powerful locos. Thus both on the regauged lines and on the existing 750mm lines, the Px48s formed the backbone of the PKP's narrow gauge motive power fleet in the postwar period.

An additional three Px48s were acquired by the PKP for the 785mm Upper Silesian narrow gauge system. Originally numbered Px48–2701–3, they were regauged to 750mm in 1965–68, becoming Px48–1925–7 and allocated to other PKP narrow gauge lines.

Seventeen 750mm gauge Px48s were rebuilt to metre gauge at the Nowy Sącz locomotive works between 1969 and 1974. They were renumbered Px48–3900–16 and worked on the metre gauge lines in north-west Poland. The rebuild was not a conspicuous success. As metre gauge locos, they were considered to be underpowered. Withdrawal took place between 1975 and the early 1980s, which meant that some of them had very short working lives in their rebuilt form. Px48–3901 has recently been restored to working order.

Wp29

	PKP–A		DRB	PKP–B
	Wp29–901	War 155/1929	99 2574	Px29–1706
	902	158/1929	2575	1701
	903	159/1929	2576	1707
	904	184/1929	2577	1704
	905	185/1929	2578	1708
	906	186/1929	2579	1705
	907	187/1929	2580	1709
	908	243/1930	2581	1702
	909	244/1930	2582	1703
	910	245/1930	2584	1710
	911	246/1930	2583	1711
	912	247/1930	—	—
	913	248/1930	—	—
	Wp29–1730	154/1929	—	—
	1731	157/1929	—	—
Wp29–910	1732	245/1930	2584	1710
	1733	188/1929	—	—
	1734	189/1929	—	—
	Wp29–4581	190/1929	—	—
	4582	191/1929	—	—
	4583	192/1929	—	—
Wp29–912	4584	247/1930	—	—
913	4585	248/1930	—	—
	Wp29–3005*	156/1929	—	—
		(760mm gauge)		

* Regauged to 750mm in 1936 and transferred to DOKP Wilno; loco presumably renumbered but to what is unknown.

Wp29 renumberings in the Soviet Union:

Wp29–4581	Tch–151	Rp–770
4582	152	771
4583	153	
4584	154	
4585	155	
Wp29–1730	Tp 1730	Tp = *Trofeyny parovos* = trophy loco)
1731?		
1732	Tch–1732†	
1733?		
1734	Wp29–1734	

† In the USSR, loco renumberings were not always consistent and it may be assumed that Tch–1732 was not the former Wp29–1732, which (supposedly) became Px29–1710.

Thirteen (or 14) locos to the Px48 design were built for industrial concerns in Poland, including four for the 785mm lines in Upper Silesia and two for the 760mm Łupków–Cisna–Moczarne forestry railway. Px48–1253–5 (Chrz 4516/1955) was preserved for many years at Cisna, but has since been moved to Sochaczew. Any further information on the others would be welcome.

A small number were exported. In 1949 ten were sent to Romania. Here they were classified as the 'Duna' class and were principally employed on the 760mm systems at Satu Mare and Tîrgu Mureş. These differed in detail from the standard PKP design, notably in the number and location of domes on the boiler and the provision of a smaller 4-wheel tender. Marginally longer and shorter than the Px48, the CFR 0–8–0s had a somewhat 'racier' appearance than their Polish counterparts; they were also slightly more powerful. It should be noted that they appeared two years before the production PKP Px48 and the 'Duna' may perhaps be considered an intermediate design.

Their CFR numbers were 764.051–60. For a long time there was some confusion over the Chrzanów works numbers of these locos. In *The Locomotives of Romania* (Malmö, 1970), C. J. Halliwell

The driver of Px48–1756 awaits the right away with a Zaniemyśl to Środa passenger train on 18 April 1990. Some crude repairs have been made to the smokebox door.
Keith Chester

Two of the three Px48s originally built for the 785mm gauge lines in Upper Silesia were in service at the very end of steam on the PKP. This view of Px48–1925, ex Px48–2703 and rebuilt in 1965, was taken at Gniezno (ng) MPD on 6 September 1989.
Keith Chester

quotes them as Chrzanów 102–111/1949, but suggests that as these numbers are too low, 2102–2111 would be more correct. These numbers, however, were allocated to Pt47–162–171. 764.056 was noted dumped at Tîrgu Mureş MPD in April 1992, fortunately still carrying all its worksplates. 107 is in fact the tender number, whilst the loco number is Chrzanów 1997/1948. None of the four other 'Duna' still extant have any worksplates, but it may be assumed that the correct numbers are Chrzanów 1992–2001/1948.

Polish sources quote 12 760mm gauge Px48s as having been exported to Jugoslavia, where they were designated class 'Sawa'. In fact these locos never reached Jugoslavia. Following Tito's political breach with the Stalinist communist block in 1948, the order was cancelled and the PKP was obliged to acquire the locos. Suitably modified and regauged to 750mm, they became class Px49 (Chrzanów 2031–40/1950). The Px49 differed from the Px48 most obviously in the provision of a three-axle tender and in being equipped with a steam brake; it was thus not fitted with the air compressors standard on the Px48. Presumably 12 locos were ordered for Jugoslavia, of which 10 were constructed before the contract was rescinded.

A further five Px48s were exported to Albania and China and here too there is some uncertainty. It is believed that Chrzanów 2166–7, 2174–5/1952 were delivered to China (762mm) and 3064/1952 (600mm) direct to Albania. Polish sources have suggested that the Chinese locos were re-exported to Albania in 1957. 2174–5 were, however, 'discovered' by enthusiasts in the mid 1980s to be still hard at work on the Yingde Mineral Railway in southern China, where they were numbered BL49 and BL50. The 'BL' prefix is thought to come from 'Bo Lan', which is the pinyin

No new motive power had been provided for the metre gauge lines in Pomerania since the 1930s and 17 Px48s were rebuilt in the mid 1960s to remedy this. Unfortunately the rebuilds were not a success. Px48–3902 was photographed at Stargard in August 1978.   *Klaus Kieper*

In 1948 Chrzanów supplied 10 type Px48s to Romania as class 'Duna'. 764.057 (Chrz 1698/1948) is seen here at Satu Mare MPD on 26 August 1974.   *Şerban Lacriţeanu*

Without the air compressors standard to the Px48, the Px49s had a somewhat neater appearance; note also the smaller six-wheel tender. This photograph of Px49–1799 was taken at Prezeworsk in 1973.
Bogdan Pokropiński

Two or three Px48s were exported to Albania and used on the 600mm Vlora–Selenice line. Chrzanów 2167/1952 was noted dumped at Dürres Shkozet MPD on 28 August 1985.
Uwe Bergmann

BL50 (Chrz 2175/1952) has evidently undergone some local modifications during its years on the Yingde Mineral Railway in Guangdong province in southern China, but it is still clearly recognisable as a Px48. September 1986.
John Athersuch

phonetic transcription of Poland in Mandarin. Equally certain is the fate of 2167, seen by Uwe Bergmann at Dürres-Shkozet (Albania) in 1985. Less clear is whether it had come to Albania direct with 3064 or via China. 2166 remains for the moment a mystery. In Albania, the Px48s were used on the 600mm Vlora–Selenice line, which would have meant the regauging of any ex-Chinese locos.

On the PKP, the Px48/9s far outlived other narrow gauge steam locomotives. But in the course of the 1980s even they began to fall victim to line closures and encroaching diesels and it was anticipated that they would all have been withdrawn by 1987–88. This fortunately did not prove to be the case. When the communist regime collapsed in 1989 and it became possible to photograph freely in Poland, two lines were still Px48 operated and attracted many visitors. On the rump of the Gnesener Kreisbahn, 1,435mm gauge freight wagons on narrow gauge transporters were worked to Witkowice and occasionally beyond. Rumours of dieselisation in the summer of 1991 proved unfounded and the service has continued, albeit increasingly infrequently and irregularly, to be operated solely by Px48s. On an equally small remnant of a once large system – the Schroader Kreisbahn – Px48s hauled frequent and well-filled passenger trains between Środa and Zaniemyśl. Thus the Px48 was the last narrow gauge steam locomotive class working scheduled passenger trains in Europe. At the time of writing (Winter 1993) the Środa branch is still Px48 worked and there has been talk of converting this into a steam museum operation. Given the parlous state of the Polish economy, this would, however, seem unlikely, though it is far from clear why the Środa branch has remained Px48 worked for so long. The PKP has at present 19 Px48s in stock and none of these are likely to be cut up. In addition several Px48/9s have already been preserved, both in Poland and abroad.

Most workings on the freight only Gniezno system are of standard gauge wagons on ng Rollwagen. Here unusually Px48–1728 passes the Gniezno city limits with a pw train consisting of 750mm gauge stock on 19 April 1990. Keith Chester

An unidentified Px48 0–8–0 hauls an early morning passenger train on the 750mm gauge Środa–Zaniemyśl line in western Poland in April 1990. Four years later this is still steam worked and is the last narrow gauge passenger service scheduled for steam haulage in Europe. Tony Eaton

On 15 September 1993, C4 7110 (Canton works no. 10 of 1971) has just been serviced at Mei Xian MPD prior to working back to Xibu.
Keith Chester

SON OF Px48?

The Chinese built C4 class 0–8–0s, illustrated above, may perhaps be the final link in the chain which began with the W–3–A back in 1927. For these locos, at least their underframes, bear a remarkable similarity to the Px48: axle spacings and wheel diameters are identical. The design evolved in the late 1960s at the Canton Motive Power Machinery Works. With Yingde and its two BL class Px48s only 150km to the north, it is hard to believe that the Canton engineers were not familiar with the type. And though we have no concrete evidence, it is also not too hard to believe that when the Chinese required something more powerful than the C2, they simply took the proven chassis of the Px48, slightly increased the size of the cylinders and topped it all off with a larger boiler and cab. That the Chinese regularly plagiarised existing (foreign) designs when building their own steam power is no secret. To this may be added the fact that the Poles provided the Chinese with full technical documentation on all the steam locos they supplied. So when the fires are finally dropped on the last PKP Px48s at Środa and Gniezno, this may not be quite the end of the story.

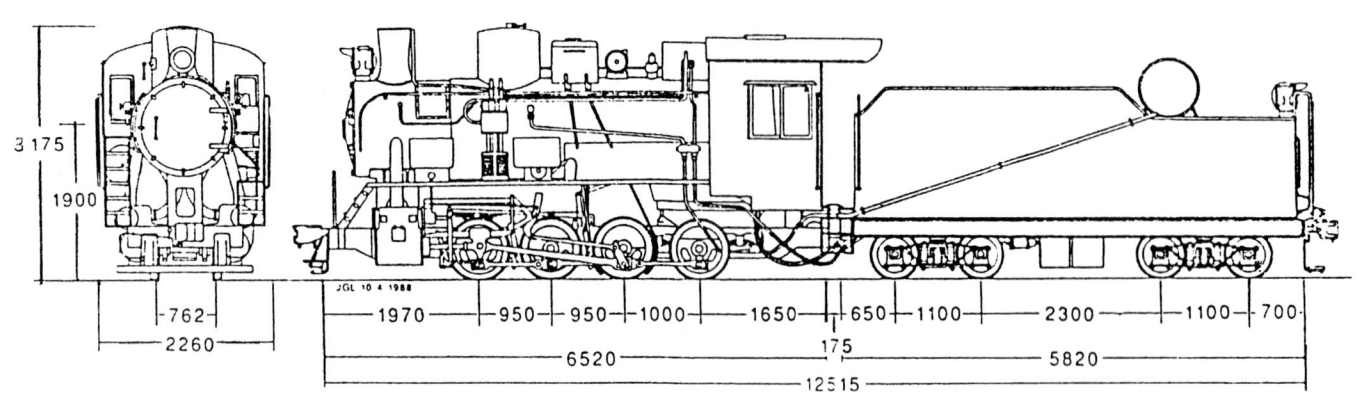

C4 Class. Guangzhou Motive Power Plant. San Shui Locomotive & Car Factory.

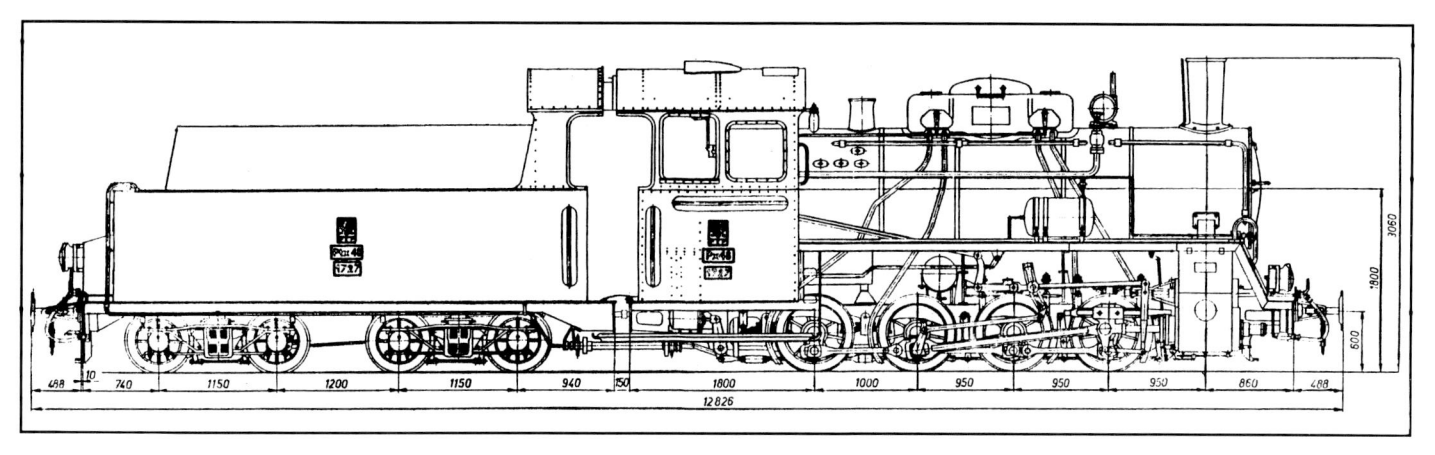

There is a large network of metre gauge lines centred on Gryfice in NW Poland; here Px48–3915 heads a passenger from Gryfice to Świelino on 16 August 1981.   Trevor Rowe

Px48 Lists

PKP No.	Builder	Works No./Year	*reb 1,000mm 1963–65*	PKP No.	Builder	Works No./Year	*reb 1,000mm 1963–65*
Px48–1721	Chrzanów	2021/1950		Px48–1737	Chrzanów	2122/1951	
1722		2022/1950	Px48–3916	1738		2123/1951	
1723		2023/1950		1739		2124/1951	
1724		2024/1950		1740		2125/1951	Px48–3900
1725		2025/1950		1741		2126/1951	
1726		2026/1950		1742		2127/1951	
1727		2027/1950	Px48–3907	1743		2128/1951	
1728		2028/1950		1744		2129/1951	Px48–3909
1729		2029/1950		1745		2130/1951	
1730		2030/1950		1746		2131/1951	
1731		2116/1951	Px48–3904	1747		2132/1951	
1732		2117/1951	Px48–3901	1748		2133/1951	
1733		2118/1951		1749		2134/1951	Px48–3902
1734		2119/1951		1750		2135/1951	Px48–3906
1735		2120/1951		1751		2246/1952	
1736		2121/1951		1752		2247/1952	

Px48 Lists *continued*

PKP No.	Builder	Works No./Year	reb 1,000mm 1963–65	PKP No.	Builder	Works No./Year	reb 1,000mm 1963–65
Px48–1753	Chrzanów	2248/1952	Px48–3913	Px48–1780	Chrzanów	3067/1954	Px48–3911
1754		2249/1952		1781		3068/1954	Px48–3912
1755		2250/1952		1782		3069/1954	Px48–3903
1756		2253/1952		1783		3070/1954	
1757		2254/1952		1784		3219/1954	
1758		2168/1952		1785		3220/1954	
1759		2169/1952		1786		3221/1954	
1760		2170/1952		1787		3222/1954	
1761		2171/1952		1788		3223/1954	
1762		2172/1952		1789		3224/1954	
1763		2173/1952	Px48–3910	1790		3225/1954	
1764		3049/1952		Px49–1791		2031/1950	
1765		3050/1952		1792		2032/1950	
1766		3051/1952	Px48–3915	1793		2033/1950	
1767		3052/1952		1794		2034/1950	
1768		3053/1952		1795		2035/1950	
1769		3054/1952	Px48–3905	1796		2036/1950	
1770		3055/1952		1797		2037/1950	
1771		3056/1952		1798		2038/1950	
1772		3057/1952		1799		2039/1950	
1773		3058/1952		1800		2040/1950	
1774		3059/1952		Px48–1901		3227/1954	
1775		3060/1952		1902		3228/1954	
1776		3061/1952	Px48–3914	1903		3233/1955	
1777		3062/1952		1904		3234/1955	
1778		3063/1952		1905		3248/1953	
1779		3066/1954	Px48–3908	1906		3236/1953	

No fewer than six Px29s have been preserved. Px29–1704 is normally one of the active locos at the Sochaczew railway museum near Warsaw. 30 April 1989.   Keith Chester

Px48 Lists continued

PKP No.	Builder	Works No./Year	PKP No.	Builder	Works No./Year	reb 785mm to 750mm
Px48–1907	Chrzanów	4508/1955	Px48–1919	Chrzanów	4507/1955	
1908		3238/1953	1920		4509/1955	
1909		3239/1953	1921		4510/1955	
1910		3244/1953	1922		4511/1955	
1911		3245/1953	1923		4512/1955	
1912		3246/1953	1924		4513/1955	
1913		3247/1953	1925		2252/1952	ex Px48–2703 reb. 1965
1914		3249/1953				
1915		3072/1952	1926		3240/1953	ex Px48–2702 reb. 1968
1916		3073/1952				
1917		3074/1952	1927		3230/1954	ex Px48–2701 reb. 1968
1918		3075/1952				

Px48s in Industry

Two lists of the Px48 known to have been constructed for industrial enterprises are available. There are some discrepancies between them and any corrections would be welcome.

List A:
Chrzanów 3229, 3231–32, 35, 37, 41–43, 4514–16/1955

List B:
Chrzanów 2251, 55/19??, 3229, 32, 35, 37, 41–43, 4514–16/1955

Px48s Exported

ROMANIA: (Type 'Duna')
CFR 764.051–060   Chrz 1992–2001/1948

ALBANIA & CHINA:
Chrzanów   2166/1952   (?)
           2167/1952   Albania
           2174/1952   China
           2175/1952   China
           3064/1952   Albania (?)

Px48–1758 blasts away from Gniezno with a freight for Witkowo on 2 January 1990.   Keith Chester

Principal Dimensions of W–3–A, Wp29, Px48 and 'Duna'

	W–3–A	Wp29	Px48	'Duna'
HP	120	180	180	—
Gauge	750mm	750mm	750mm	760mm
Axle loading	4.8t	5.62t	5.5t	5.5t
Cylinder diameter	310mm	320mm	320mm	320mm
Stroke	320mm	360mm	360mm	360mm
Wheel diameter	650mm	750mm	750mm	750mm
Total wheel base	2,300mm	2,900mm	2,900mm	2,900mm
Boiler pressure	13bar/185psi	13bar/185psi	13bar/185psi	13bar/185psi
Total heating surface	—	51.4m^2	53.8m^2	—
Water capacity	2.5m^2	6m^2	6m^2	—
Coal capacity	0.9m^2	4m^2	4m^2	—
Weight (empty)	15t	19.7t	20t	20t
Weight (in service)	19.4t	21.8t	22t	22t
Adhesive weight	19.4t	21.8t	22t	22t
Total length of loco	5,900mm	7,000mm	6,998mm	7,360mm
Height	3,000mm	3,100mm	3,060mm	3,000mm
Width	1,940mm	2,180mm	2,240mm	2,120mm
Minimum radius	20m	35m	35m	—
Maximum speed	30kmph	35kmph	35kmph	35kmph

On the last day of 1989, Px48–1756 is prepared for its next turn of duty at Środa MPD. Keith Chester

THE HRONEC FORESTRY RAILWAY

Keith Chester

Slovakia has always been the poor relation of the Czech lands of Bohemia and Moravia; whilst the latter had become the industrial heartland of the Austro–Hungarian Empire by the beginning of the twentieth century, the province to the east, which belonged to the Hungarian Monarchy, was impoverished and lived mainly off its agriculture. Though Slovakia was rich in minerals and timber, neither could be properly exploited as relatively few roads and railways had as yet been constructed. Timber was felled only where it could be floated down a river – an inefficient and unsatisfactory method of transport; for their part, the mining and smelting industries had reached the limits of their development without improvements in the transport system.

A feature of the HLŽ until 1962 was the operation of regular passenger trains, using, as can be seen here, bogie stock. Judging by the clothes worn by the passengers this could be a sunday or holiday excursion train. 0–8–0T no. 5 was built by Sigl in 1909 and scrapped in 1947.
Collection: ČHŽ

No. 4 was a classic Budapest product and was photographed in the 1920s. The plate on the lower cab sides bears the legend C.H.L.D. which stands for 'Čierno Hronská Lesná Dráha' or Black River Forestry Railway – the old name of the railway.
Collection: ČHŽ

Between the turn of the century and the outbreak of war in 1914, more than 20 narrow gauge agricultural, industrial and, above all, forestry railways were built to alleviate these problems; by 1929 the number had grown to more than 50 such privately-owned lines. Even more were projected, but fell victim first to the economic crisis of 1929–34 and then growing competition from road transport.

By 1938 almost half of the forestry railways had either been nationalised or were being administered by the *Československý štátne lesy* (= Czechoslovak State Forests). In 1937 this organisation was responsible for 486km of track, 29 steam, two electric and four diesel locomotives, as well as 749 wagons. After the communists came to power in 1948, all the remaining forestry railways were taken over by the state and came under the aegis of this organisation.

Perhaps the largest and most important of all the forestry railways in Slovakia was that at Hronec – the *Hronecká Lesná Železnica*. In September 1903, the MÁV opened its standard gauge line between Zvolen and Červená Skala in one of the most backward regions of Slovakia. With the exception of a 4km line from Podbrezová to Hronec (1910), calls for additional branches to promote the economic development of the area were ignored. Private interests, principally the forest owners, therefore took it upon themselves to provide their own railway and in 1908 a 760mm line was built between Hronec and Čierny Balog. Steam locomotives were introduced in 1910 and thereafter the system rapidly expanded.

By 1938 it had reached its maximum length of 131.98km and was employing 115 people. The main facilites of the railway were at Hronec, where there was a repair works, a loco depot and exchange sidings with the ČSD. The railway was originally administered from Čierny Balog, where a large sawmill was erected. As the maximum gradients of one in 14 and minimum curves of 60m radius would suggest, the railway ran through hilly and wild countryside. It is generally considered to have been the most scenic forestry railway in Slovakia.

In addition, it was also one of the busiest. Yet, despite the large quantities of timber (and until 1962 passengers) it transported and the inadequate roads in its lonely valleys, even the Hronec Forestry Railway could not resist the onslaught of

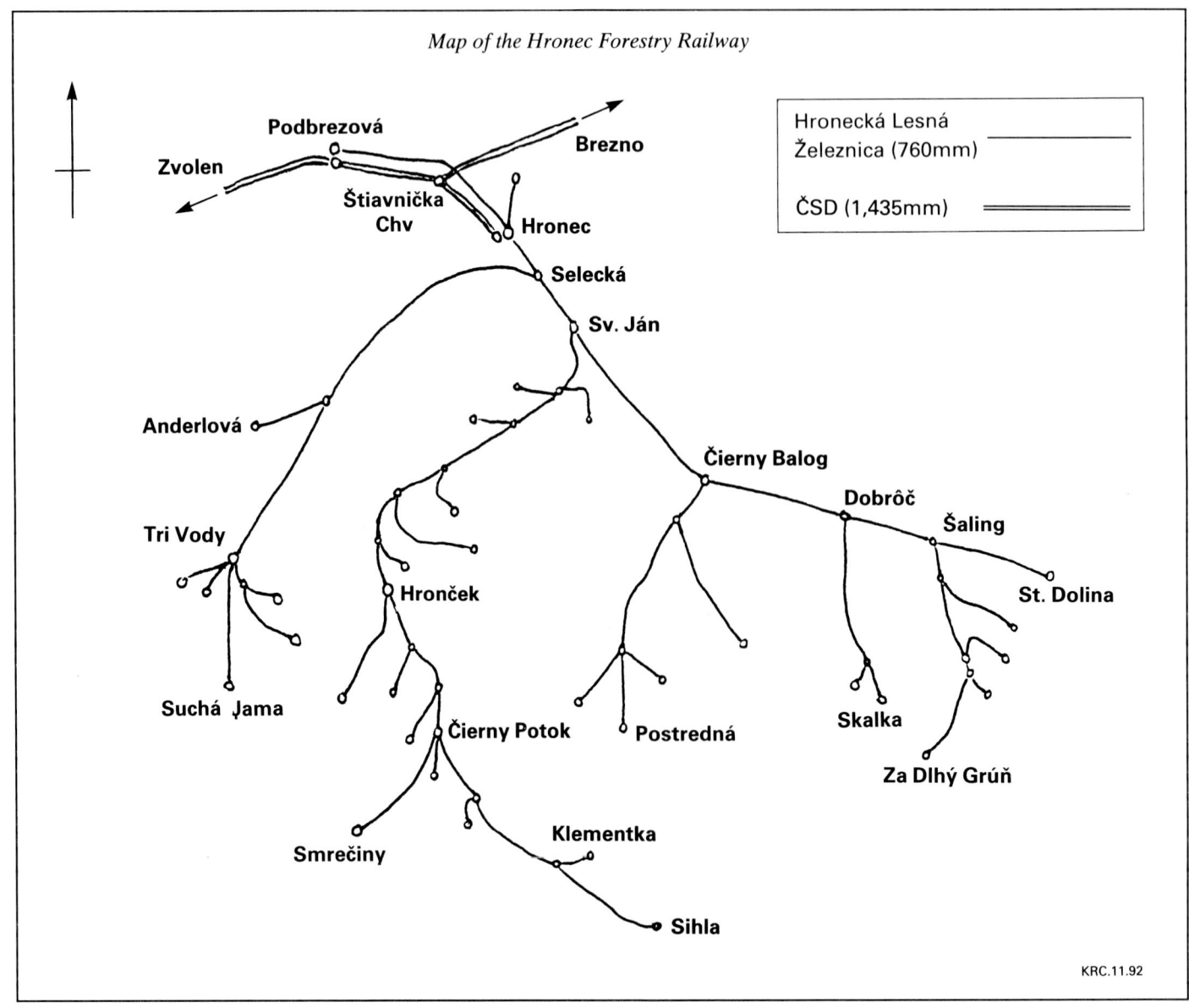

Map of the Hronec Forestry Railway

'progress' in the form of the lorry. In 1974, there were still 100km of the railway in use; by the end of the decade, only approximately 30km remained. As the last active forestry railway in Slovakia, it was reduced to a daily train between Čierny Balog and Hronec and irregular workings down the stumps of the branches. Not surprisingly, many railway enthusiasts made the pilgrimage to this remote part of Slovakia and the final years of the line are well documented. The Hronec Forestry Railway was closed on 31 December 1982.

Fortunately this was not the end of the story. That same year, pressure from enthusiasts and the youth conservation movement *Strom Zivota* led to the railway being declared a national monument. This was in fact the first notable victory for the 'greens' in Slovakia. In subsequent years working parties began the long rehabilitation of the railway and in the spring of 1992 their efforts were rewarded with the re-opening of the line from Čierny Balog to the loop at Sanské. The railway was re-opened to Hronec on 1 May 1993 and ultimately museum trains will operate over 17kms. Four of the original locos are currently at Čierny Balog.

In the early years, motive power on the Slovakian forestry lines came mainly from the Budapest works or various German manufacturers. Neither is particularly surprising, given the predominance of German loco builders in Central Europe and the fact that Slovakia was part of Hungary. In the 1920s and 1930s both Škoda and ČKD produced various standard and narrow gauge locos for industry, including eight 0–8–0Ts (ČKD 1441–3/1928 and 1540–4/1930) for the Slovakian forestry railways, one of which worked at Hronec for more than 30 years.

U34₉₀₁ worked at Hronec for just over 50 years; this photograph was taken in 1967 near the end of its active career. In the mid 1970s it was moved to the museum at Vychylovka where it is still occasionally steamed.
Jiri Joachymstál

Many Budapest 0–8–0Ts of type 70 (see page 19) were supplied to forestry railways throughout Central Europe. U46₉₀₁ was built in 1942 to an enlarged and improved design. Upon withdrawal it was plinthed at Brezno MPD but in 1993 was returned to Čierny Balog for restoration to working order. Čierny Balog, 1967.
Jiri Joachymstál

By the summer of 1982, the Hronec Forestry Railway was only six months away from closure. Traffic levels were low but it was possible for photographers to 'chase' a loaded train from the sawmill at Čierny Balog to Hronec, where the timber was transhipped onto ČSD wagons. On 9 August 1982 the sole train of the day was hauled by no. 1 (ČKD 2609/1948). Note the hosepipe suspended on the rear of the coal bunker. When the loco took water, this was simply dropped into a convenient stream and the water pumped into the loco's tanks.

Čierny Balog . . . Hans Hufnagel

Drifting down to Hronec from Čierny Balog . . . Hans Hufnagel

Shunting at Hronec . . . Hans Hufnagel

Lunchbreak at Hronec . . . Hans Hufnagel

77

U36₉₀₁

Perhaps the most curious of Hronec's locomotives was its no. 7, later U36₉₀₁. It only spent two (less than active) years on the line and was probably one of the least successful locos to have operated there.

Its origins are quite bizarre. On 1 April 1936, the state forestry authority took over from the ČSD the 760mm gauge Teresva–Neresnice line in Podkarpatská Rus. This was part of Czechoslovakia until 1939 and is now in Ukraine. Although the forestry authority was able to purchase the rolling stock of this railway from the ČSD, the latter refused to sell any of the locos, of which it was itself desperately short. This presented the forestry authorities at Teresva with a problem: the most modern locos suitable for use on forestry railways were the 0–8–0Ts of 1927–28 with a maximum speed of 20kmph; on the other hand, they were also required to maintain passenger services which needed rather speedier locos.

The forestry authorities therefore entered into discussions with ČKD for the construction of a loco which could be used on passenger services at Teresva; the forestry railways at Hronec and Liptovský Hrádok also expressed interest in this project. In 1937 an order was placed for two 90HP 0–6–0Ts. These were allocated works numbers 1801 and 1802 and given the project name 'Ustcorna' (the seat of the HQ of the Teresva railway). Technically the design was conventional, save it would have carried the first (partially) welded boiler in Czechoslovakia.

Construction proceeded slowly and then was overtaken by political events. In 1939, Podkarpatská Rus was annexed by Hungary and the order was cancelled. Many of the components for the locos, including the boilers, already existed, but had not yet been assembled.

This, however, was not the end of the story. On 30 April 1940, the Banská Bystrica forestry authority placed an order with ČKD for a 120HP 0–6–2T (ČKD number 2135 and project name 'Bystrice'). Because of the war, construction of the loco took nearly six years and every effort was made to use as many existing components as possible. Thus many of the leading dimensions correspond to the narrow gauge C600/120 0–6–0s built by ČKD for the German army or the 1435mm gauge CN600 'Hanibal' type. The regulator and steam brake, for example, were taken direct from the C600/120, whilst the cab and tanks were lightly modified versions of those of the 'Hanibal'. The frames, wheels and valve gear came from the abandoned 'Ustcorna' 0–6–2T. The loco was finally completed at the end of 1946 and was sent to Hronec in early 1947.

The new loco, by now almost 10 years in gestation, was given the number 7, later changed to U36₉₀₁. Unfortunately it had not been worth the wait. Originally conceived as a passenger loco and for well-maintained track, the loco was ill-suited to the needs and conditions of a forestry railway. It was prone to derailment and its relatively large wheels of 820mm diameter rendered it unsuitable for heavy timber trains. It was therefore restricted to hauling passenger trains between Hronec and Dobroč.

It must therefore have been with some relief at Hronec that no. 7 was hired for a short time to the forestry railway at Liptovský Hrádok in 1949. Here it spread the track and was equally unpopular. It was soon exchanged for an older O&K 0–8–0T from the Oscadnica forestry railway. With its badly maintained track and sharp curves, Oscadnica was an even less likely venue for the successful operation of U36₉₀₁ than Hronec and Liptovský Hrádok.

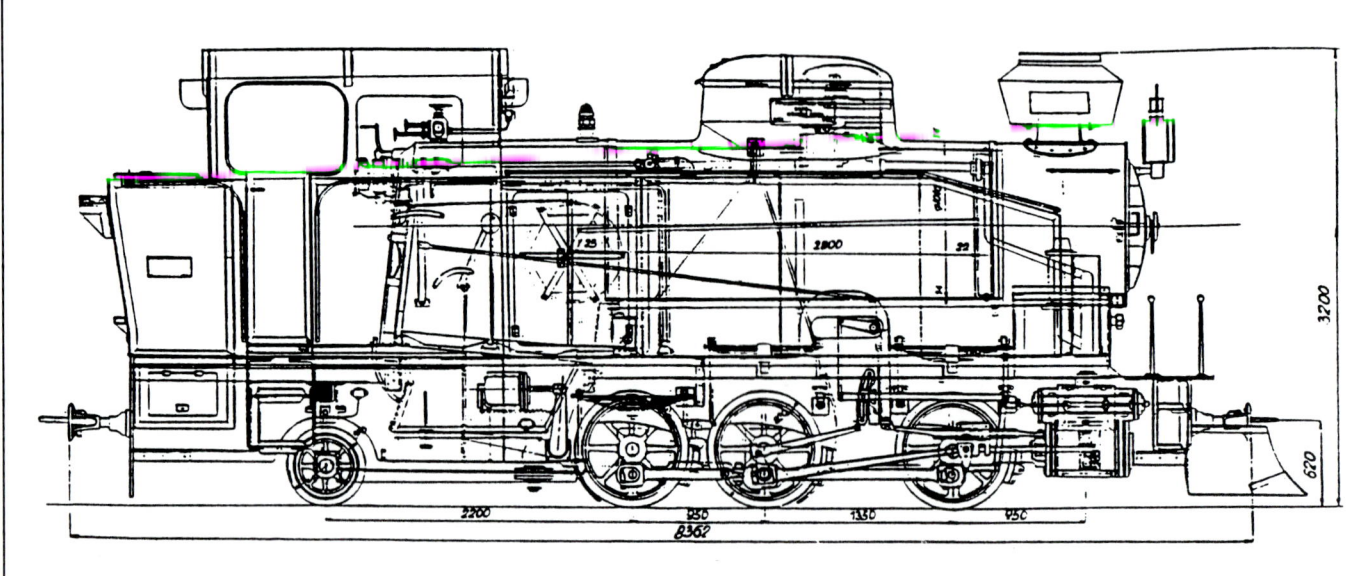

U36₉₀₁ as originally built

U36₉₀₁ continued

In 1956 the decision was taken to rebuild the loco to make it more powerful and able to negotiate curves of 40m radius. The diameter of the coupled wheels was reduced to 700mm (incidentally that of the original 'Ustcorna' design), whilst the Krauss-Helmholtz truck was replaced by a four-wheel bogie. The rebuild was, however, not a success and U36₉₀₁ did little work thereafter. In 1961 its boiler was sold to the sawmill at Ruzomberok and the rest of this ill-starred loco was scrapped.

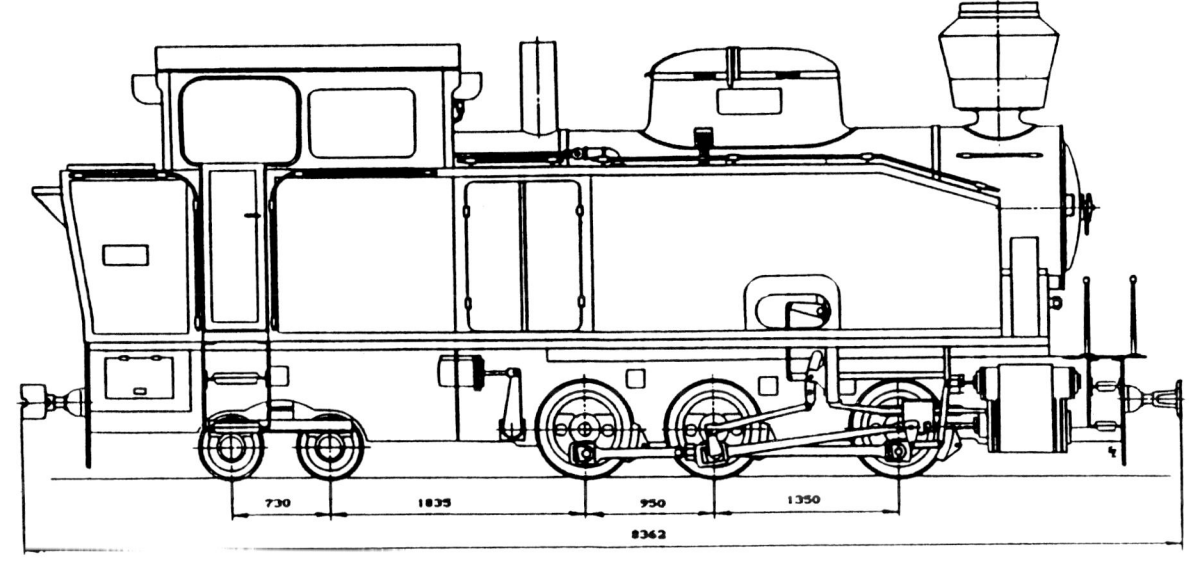

U36₉₀₁ as rebuilt in 1956

When ČKD resumed building locomotives in 1947–48, it developed a wide range of industrial designs for various gauges. Among these was an 0–6–0T, using saturated steam, which was first introduced in 1948 and classified type C760/90–d. As this implies, this was an 0–6–0T for 760mm gauge developing 90HP; the 'd' stands for *drevo* (= wood), i.e. the locos were designed for wood firing. Typical of locos built for forestry lines, it had outside frames. It was fitted with Heusinger-Walschaerts valve gear, with drive on the rear axle. The boiler was all-welded, with a copper firebox; braking was manual or steam operated.

Six locomotives of this type were built for use on the forestry railways in Slovakia (ČKD 2607–12/1948) and a further 10 (ČKD 2616–25/1948) for 750mm gauge were exported to the Soviet Union where they found use on peat railways. Nine similar locos with superheat were constructed in 1950 (ČKD 2491–99) for export to Jugoslavia but fell foul of the ideological divide in the socialist world and remained in Czechoslovakia. Five of the six C760/90–d built for Slovakian forestry railways worked at one time or another at Hronec and three of them are now preserved there. In latter years the railway also used a few diesels, notably three Bo-Bo's acquired from Raba in 1961.

ČKD built 10 750mm gauge 0–6–0Ts for export to the Soviet Union in 1948. They were identical to the locos used at Hronec.
Collection: Peeter Klaus

Principal Dimensions of the C760/90–d

Gauge	mm	760
Cylinder bore	mm	275
Piston stroke	mm	360
Diameter of coupled wheels	mm	700
Rigid wheelbase	mm	2,200
Total wheelbase	mm	2,200
Steam pressure	atm.	13
Grate area	sq. metres	1.02
Heating surface, water side:		
firebox	sq. metres	4.06
tubes	sq. metres	25.22
total	sq. metres	29.28
Distance between tube plates	mm	2,200
Water tank capacity	cu. metres	1.5
Peat container capacity	cu. metres	1.3
Weight of locomotive, empty	kg	13,000
Weight of locomotive, adhesive	kg	17,000
Weight of locomotive, service	kg	17,000
Rated tractive force $p \dfrac{d^2 \cdot s \cdot i}{D^2}$	kg	3,880
Length of locomotive (over couplers)	mm	6,782
Overall width	mm	2,150
Overall height	mm	3,000
Maximum permissible speed	km per hour	20
Minimum radius of track	metres	30

(Taken from 1955 ČKD catalogue)

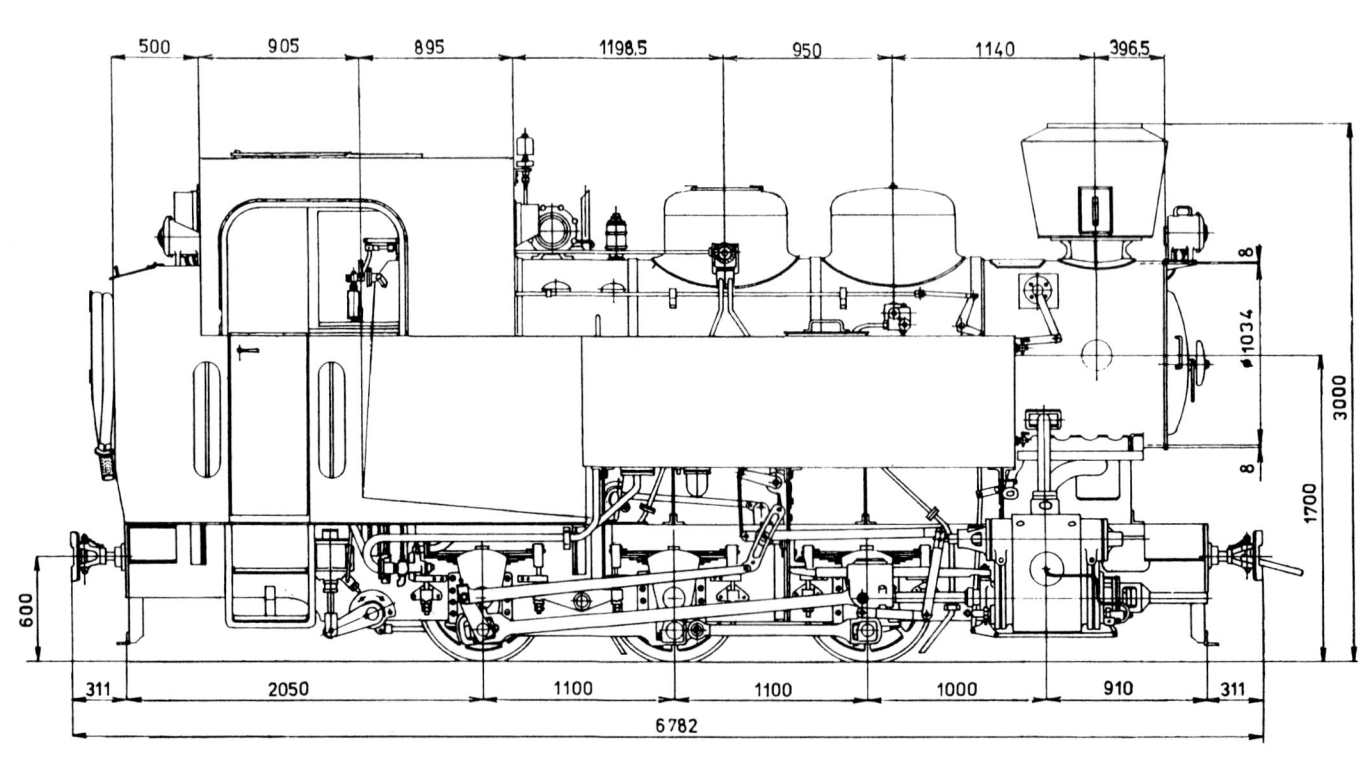

ČKD supplied six type C760/90–d 0–6–0Ts to various forestry railways in Slovakia in 1948; not surprisingly these modern engines were amongst the last active steam locos on Slovakia's forestry lines.

The Steam Locomotives of the HLŽ

a	b	c					
1	U33₉₀₁	–	0–6–0T	Jung	2598	1918	1952 to Trencianska Tepla
2	—	—	0–6–0T	Bp	2165	1909	1925 to Víglaš
3	U34₉₀₁	2″	0–6–0T	Bp	2282	1909	c. 1977 to Vychylovka for preservation
4	U34₉₀₃	—	0–6–0T	Bp	2819	1911	acquired 1923; 1954 to Spiska Nova Ves
5	U44₉₀₁	—	0–8–0T	Sigl	4983	1909	acquired 1922; scrapped 1947
6	U45₉₀₁	4″	0–8–0T	ČKD	1544	1930	withdrawn c. 1965
—	U35₉₀₁	1″	0–6–0T	ČKD	2609	1948	acquired 1949; preserved at Čierny Balog
—	—	3″	0–6–0T	ČKD	2608	1948	acquired 1954; scrapped 1980
—	U35₉₀₂	5″	0–6–0T	ČKD	2611	1948	preserved in working order at Čierny Balog
—	U46₉₀₁	6″	0–8–0T	Bp	5277	1942	1973(?) preserved at Brezno MPD; 1993 to Čierny Balog for for restoration
7	U36₉₀₁	—	0–6–2T	ČKD	2135	1947	1949 to Povaskou
—	U35₉₀₃	7″	0–6–0T	ČKD	2610	1948	acquired 1954; preserved at Čierny Balog
—	—	—	0–8–0	O&K	11042	1925	acquired 1952; 1954 to Zarnovice
—	U17₅₄₈	—	0–6–0T	ČKD	2612	1948	acquired 1980; preserved at Víglaš

a = original number

b = numbering scheme used from 1931, similar to ČSD system

c = numbering scheme adopted c. 1960

U17₅₄₈ only arrived on the Hronec Forestry Railway in 1980, but can have done very little work there. Looking very forlorn, it was photographed dumped at Hronec in August 1982. It was subsequently plinthed at Víglaš, where there had once been a large forestry railway.
Hans Hufnagel

THE NARROW GAUGE LINES OF THE ROMANIAN STATE RAILWAYS

Şerban Lacriţeanu

The first narrow gauge line constructed by the CFR was from Bacău to Piatra Neamţ. It was metre gauge and opened on 2 February 1885. Motive power was in the form of four 0–6–0Ts supplied by Couillet. In 1892 this line was rebuilt to standard gauge and its permanent way used in the construction of the forestry railway at Tarcău.

The CFR opened a second narrow gauge railway, also metre gauge, on 25 July 1888; this was between Crasna and Dobrina (Huşi). This initially used two similar Couillet 0–6–0Ts, which were joined by the four from the Bacău line upon its conversion to 1,435mm in 1892. 35 years later, the Crasna–Dobrina railway in turn was also converted to standard gauge (on 15 April 1937) and all the locos scrapped, save 001 LESPEZI which was moved to the railway museum at Bucureşti-Nord. Sadly it was destroyed, along with other preserved rolling stock, in a heavy Allied bombing raid in April 1944. Two secondhand Krauss 0–4–0Ts were also acquired for use on this line. Following Romania's declaration of war on Germany in August 1916, they were requisitioned by the Romanian army and used in the construction of a 60km metre gauge line through the Valea Bistriţei, parts of which were later operated as a forestry railway.

0–6–0T LETEA (Couillet 784/1884), originally constructed for the 1,000mm gauge railway from Bacău to Piatra Neamţ, was transferred to the Crasna–Huşi line in 1892.
Collection: Şerban Lacriţeanu

On 14 April 1937, 005 CRASNA performs the last rites at Huşi with the final narrow gauge train to Crasna. The following day the railway was converted to standard gauge.
Collection: Şerban Lacriţeanu

Metre gauge 001 LESPEZI and standard gauge 0-6-0 no. 620 MURGENI (FB 738/1890) were photographed at Halta Crețești on 14 April 1937. MURGENI is now preserved at București Nord.
Collection: Șerban Lacrițeanu

001	LESPEZI	0-6-0T	Couillet	781/1884
002	DOCHIA			782/1884
003	HANGU			783/1884
004	LETEA			784/1884
005	CRASNA			904/1887
006	DOBRINA			905/1887
007	DOCOLINA	0-4-0T	Kr	??/??
008	BALȚ-TEȘTI			??/??

Romania expanded greatly as a result of the collapse of the Austro-Hungarian Empire at the end of the World War I. On 1 December 1918, Transylvania became part of Romania. This was formerly recognised by the 1920 Treaty of Trianon, which also marks the date of the CFR's official takeover of these former Hungarian lines. Among these were five 760mm narrow gauge lines which had previously been operated by the MÁV.

(1) SATU MARE

Company: MÁV—Szatmár-Bikszádi HÉV (SzB)
Szatmár-Erdödi HÉV (SzÉZ)

Lines:

Ghilvaci–Ardud–Ardusat	67.4km	Opened	04.10.1893
Ardud–Ardusat		Closed	29.06.1976
Ardusat–Șomcuța Mare	17km	Opened	24.03.1895
		Closed	27.05.1972
Satu Mare–Bicsad	51.6km	Opened	20.04.1906
		Regauged	28.05.1988
Satu Mare–Ardud	27.73km	Opened	14.06.1900
		Closed	31.05.1975

By 1993 only the 18km between Ghilvaci and Ardud were still operated by the CFR, with a daily service of three return mixeds.

Original motive power:

				Remarks
396,001	0-6-2T	Bp	1403/1899	1918 CFR; 1940 MÁV; 1944 CFR
396,002			1404/1899	1918 CFR
490,001	0-8-0T		1846/1906	SzB 6967 'ROBERT', 1916 Steinbeisbahn 33
490,002			1847/1906	SzB 6968; 1924 CFR

A very clean 'Duna' type 0-8-0, no. 764.051 (Chrz 1992/1948), awaits departure at Crucisor on the Satu Mare system. 20 September 1966.
Trevor Rowe

490,003		2078/1908	1918 SHS 490.003
490,004		2083/1908	1918 CFR
490,005		2501/1910	1917 Steinbeisbahn 34
490,006		2502/1910	1924 CFR
490,018		3105/1912	1916 Steinbeisbahn 35
490,019		3106/1912	1918 SHS 490.019

Locomotives used after 1960:

				Remarks
764.050 –059	0–8–0	Chrz	1992–2001/ 1948	1950–74 Satu Mare
764.001	0–8–0T	Schw	8299/1923	1972 Reşiţa Museum
764.014		Res	381/1937	wd Satu Mare 1974
764.103		Schw	8389/1923	1972 Reşiţa Museum
764.152		U23A	514/1949(?)	
764.410		Res	1419/1958	ex CFI; 1991 pres Satu Mare MPD
4013		Bp	3803/1915	ex kkHB 4013; wd Satu Mare 1975

Schwartzkopff supplied eight of these rather ungainly 0–8–0Ts to the CFR in 1923 (works numbers 8299–8306); by June 1974, 764.007 was dumped at Sibiu. Klaus Kieper

(2) TÎRGU MUREŞ

Company: Marostordai HÉV

Lines:

Tîrgu Mureş–Praid	82.6km	Opened	31.01.1915
Băile Sovata–Praid	8.198km	Closed	24.03.1975
Band–Mihesul de Cîmpie	27.748km	Opened	31.01.1915
Tîrgu Mureş–Iuda	73.958km	Opened	31.01.1915
Iuda–Lechinţa	16.412km	Opened	15.12.1941

Today this is the most extensive narrow gauge system still in operation on the CFR. The section between Tîrgu Mureş and Band is the most scenic. Here the line crosses the Band hills, climbing steeply from Tîrgu Mureş (306m) before dropping to 303m at Band. Just how severe these grades are is shown from the 1960 timetable in which 1h 55mins was required for the 27km from Tîrgu Mureş to Band. Locos working the southern branch to Băile Sovata also face steep grades, with the summit at Cîmpul

Reşiţa built a further 10 0–8–0Ts in 1937. They differed slightly from the earlier German locomotives.
Collection: Şerban Lacriţeanu

Cetatii. Here there was until 1991 a connection with the CFF line of the same name, thereby making the small halt of Cîmpul Cetatii the only place in Romania where a CFF loco could be seen on the CFR and CFR wagons on the CFF!

Original motive power:

				Remarks
490,020	0–8–0T	Bp	3153/1914	1918 SHS 490.020
490,021			3154/1914	1924 CFR
490,022			3155/1914	1918 SHS 490.022
490,023			3156/1914	1924 CFR; 1940 MÁV; 1944 USSR
490,024			3157/1914	1918 SHS 490.024
490,025			3158/1914	1918 SHS 490.025
490,026			3159/1914	1924 CFR
490,027			3160/1914	1924 CFR; 1940 MÁV; 1944 CFR
490,028			3161/1914	1924 CFR
490,029			3162/1914	1918 MÁV
490,030			3163/1914	1918 MÁV
490,031			3164/1914	1918 SHS 490.031

Locomotives used after 1960:

				Remarks
764.003	0–8–0T	Schw	8301/1923	wd Tîrgu Mureş 1981
764.004			8302/1923	wd Tîrgu Mureş 1975
764.053	0–8–0	Chrz	1994/1948	pres in wo 1993
764.056			1997/1948	1990 to Tîrgu Mureş
764.113	0–8–0T	Res	386/1937	wd Tîrgu Mureş 1974
764.153		U23A	519/1949	1949–93 Tîrgu Mureş
764.155			/1949	1949–89 Tîrgu Mureş
764.156			517/1949	1949–89 Tîrgu Mureş
764.157			523T/1949	1949–93 Tîrgu Mureş
764.158			524/1949	1949–89 Tîrgu Mureş
764.159			525/1949	pres in wo 1993
764.160			526/1949	1949–93 Tîrgu Mureş
764.201–9	0–8–0	U23A	/1949	1949–70 Tîrgu Mureş
of which:				
764.203			535/1949	1949–93 Tîrgu Mureş; to be restored to wo 1994
764.206			538/1949	1992 plinthed Tîrgu Mureş MPD

In 1949, the Uzinele '23 August', Bucureşti, constructed a final batch of 10 0–8–0Ts; though heavier, the design still clearly owed much to the 1923 Schwartzkopff version. Tîrgu Mureş, 20 September 1965.
Alfred Luft

764.159 crosses the River Mureş near Cristeşti Mureş on 13 October 1969.
Werner Fritthum

764.403	0–8–0T	O&K	5842/1912	ex CFF Hodoşa; 1968 Tîrgu Mureş; wd 1975
IVK 148	0–4–4–0T	Hart	3211/1909	1969 Tîrgu Mureş; wd 1974
396.002	0–6–2T	Bp	1404/1899	1968 Tîrgu Mureş; wd 1974
397.001	0–6–2T	WrN	3630/1893	1968 Tîrgu Mureş; wd 1974
4001	0–8–0T	Bp	3094/1914	ex kkHB 4001; 1968 Tîrgu Mureş; wd 1972
4002			3095/1914	ex kkHB 4002; 1968 Tîrgu Mureş; wd 1974
4006			3629/1914	ex kkHB 4006; 1968 Tîrgu Mureş; wd 1974
4013			3803/1914	ex kkHB 4013; 1968–71 Tîrgu Mureş

(3) SIBIU

Company: Segesvár-Szentágotai HÉV

Lines:

Sighişoara–Agnita	47km	Opened	17.11.1898
		Closed	31.04.1965
Sibiu–Cornăţel–Agnita	62km	Opened	27.09.1910
Cornăţel–Vurpăr	13km	Opened	27.10.1910

This line linked the valley of the Tîrnavu Mare with the Olt valley and the Valea Hîrtibaciului. The steepest gradient was between Brădeni and Apold. In the days of steam, the 10km between these two stations were booked to take one hour! When the line was first opened, the passenger stock was not provided with any toilet facilities. When the train halted at a station, the guard announced 'One minute *pipi*' or 'Five minutes *caca*'! No translation is necessary.

Even in the late 1960s the Sibiu system was home to some antique ng motive power. These two classic 0–6–0s were photographed at Sibiu on 15 September 1966. Trevor Rowe

389.001 (WrN 3061/1885), originally supplied to the Taraczvölgyi Vasút, is seen here at the head of train 2273 between Cornăţel and Caşolţ on 5 September 1967. Alfred Luft

Today, just as at Tîrgu Mureş, it is still possible in winter to see narrow gauge steam locos in regular service at Sibiu, albeit as heating units dragged behind a diesel. Progress!

Original motive power:			Remarks
1 'APOR'	0–6–0 WrN	3896/1896	1918 SHS 388.001
2 'SZENTÁGOTA'		3897/1896	1918 CFR 388.002; 1940 MÁV; 1944 CFR; 1974 pres Sighişoara
3 'SEGESVÁR'		3898/1896	1918 SHS 388.003

Original motive power:			Remarks
490,002	0–8–0T Bp	2425/1909	1918 CFR
492,003		2426/1909	1918 CFR
492,004		2427/1909	1924 CFR; 1940 MÁV
492,005		2428/1909	1924 CFR; 195? CFF 764–005
492,006		2429/1909	1918 CFR; 1940 MÁV
492,007		2430/1909	1918 MÁV
492,008		2431/1909	1918 CFR; 1950 CFF 764–316

388.002 was one of three 0–6–0s built by Wiener Neustadt in 1896 for the opening of the Sighişoara and Agnita line. On 5 September 1967, it was making a smoky passage along the main street of Agnita. Today it is plinthed at Sighişoara.   Alfred Luft

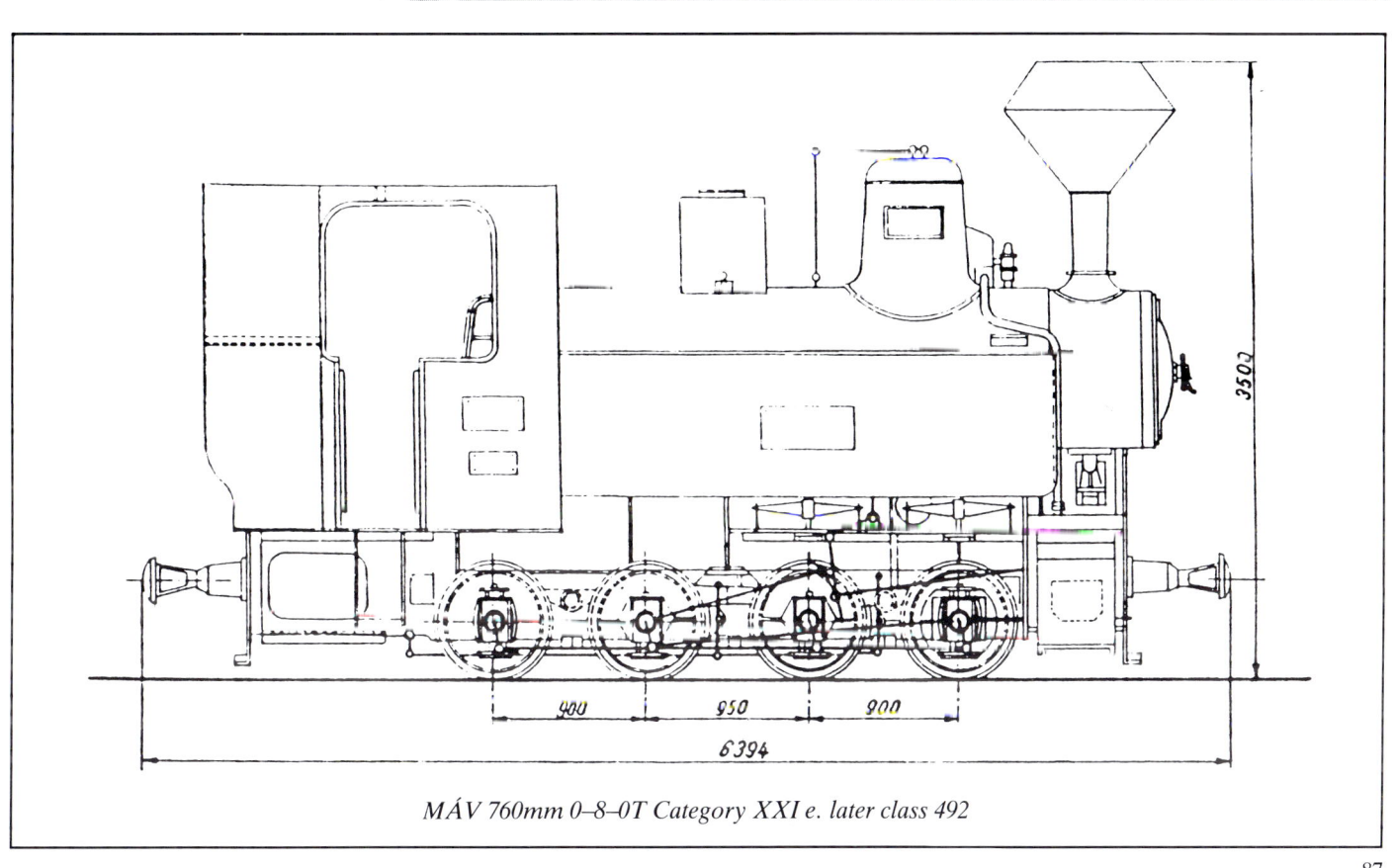

MÁV 760mm 0–8–0T Category XXI e. later class 492

Actiengesellschaft der Locomotivfabrik vorm. G. Sigl in Wr.-Neustadt.

Blatt 120.

Sechskuppler mit Tender, 0.760 Mtr. Spurweite.

Für die Marmaroser Salzbahn.

Fabr. Nr. 3554 3621 3763
1891 1892 1894

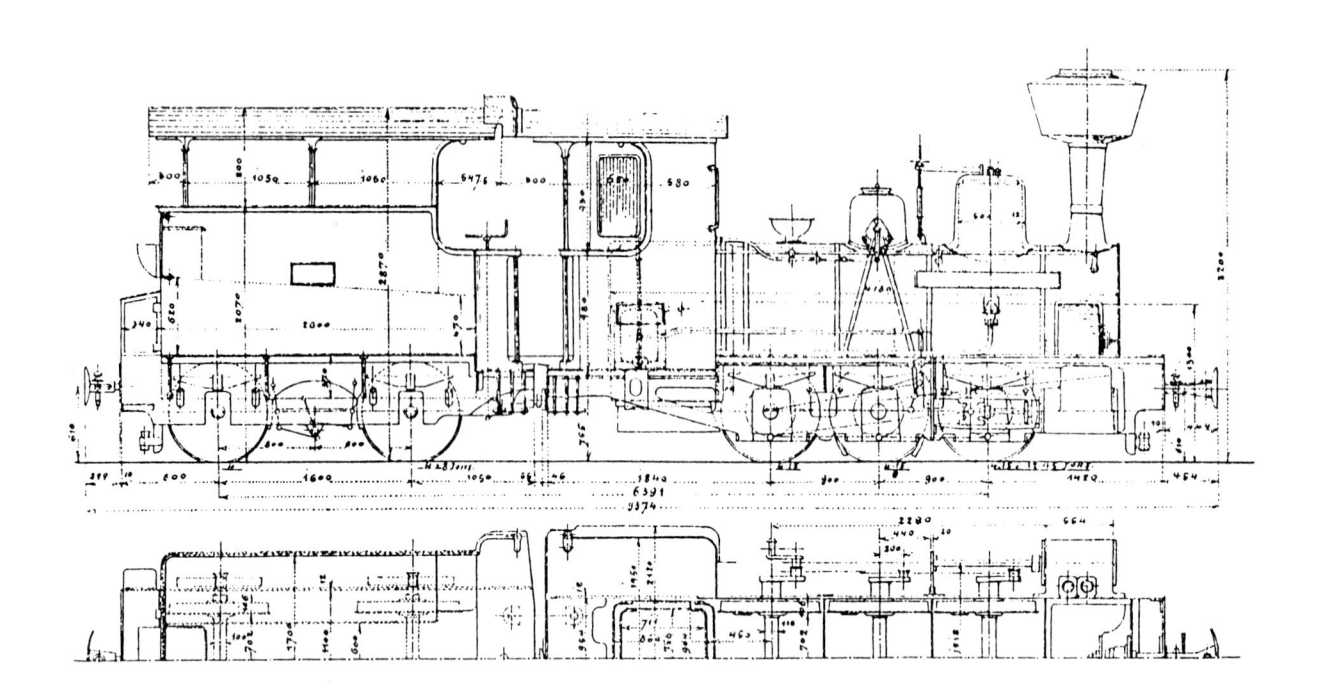

Maschine.

Effectiver Dampfdruck	12	Klgr.
Diameter des cylind. Kessels	0.840	Mtr.
Blechstärke desselben	0.011	"
Anzahl Siederohre	78	Stück
Länge derselben	2.700	Mtr.
Diameter derselben	0.046	"
Heizfläche derselben	30.4	□Mtr.
" der Box	2.6	"
" total	33.0	"
Rostfläche	0.5	"
Cylinder-Diameter	0.250	Mtr.
Kolbenhub	0.400	"
Triebrad-Diameter	0.810	"
Grösste Höhe der Maschine	3.200	Mtr.
Gewicht d. Maschine, leer	11.0	Tons
" " " im Dienste	12.45	"
Zugkraft 2×0.65	2.400	Klgr.

Tender.

Rad-Diameter	0.810	Mtr.
Radstand	1.600	"
Grösste Länge	3.804	"
" Breite	2.024	"
" Höhe	2.870	"
Inhalt des Wasserkastens	3.0	Cub.-Mtr.
" " Brennstoffraumes	2.0	"
Gewicht des Tenders, leer	4.3	Tons
" " " im Dienste	8.0	"

Collection: Pascal Pontremoli

389,001	0–6–0	WrN	3061/1885	ex Taraczvölgyi Vasút 'TARACZVÖLGY'; 1973 pres Sibiu MPD	764.007		8305/1923	1968–72 Sibiu
					764.012	Res	379/1937	1968–72 Sibiu
					764.013		380/1937	1968–72 Sibiu
389,002			3062/1885	ex Taraczvölgyi Vasút 'TEREBESPATAK'	764.015″		1086/1953	1962 ex CFI; 1992 pres TCR Bucureşti
1–3554			3554/1891	ex 'MARAMUREŞ 1'; 1984 pres Braşov MPD	764.102	Schw	8388/1923	1966 Sibiu
					764.106″	Res	/1953	ex CFI
2–3621			3621/1892	ex 'MARAMUREŞ 2'; wd 1975	764.109″		/1953	ex CFI; 1968–74 Sibiu
					764.155	U23A	/1949	1993 in service for winter train heating
3–3763			3763/1894	ex 'MARAMUREŞ 3'; wd 1975	764.156		517/1949	1993 in service for winter train heating
4–3659	0–8–0T	Maff	3659/1910	ex 'MARAMUREŞ 4'; wd 1975	764.158		524/1949	1993 in service for winter train heating
Locomotives used after 1960:					764.201	0–8–0	534/1949	1993 Sibiu
399.104	0–6–0T	Bp	2158/1910	ex Borszavölgyi HÉV 23; 1965–72 Sibiu	764.202		538/1949	1993 Sibiu
					764.205		528/1949	1993 in service for special trains
6845	0–6–2T	Bors	6845/1908	ex Huszko, Lozinsky & Co, Kiev; pres Sibiu MPD	764.207		532/1949	1993 Sibiu
764.006	0–8–0T	Schw	8304/1923	1968–72 Sibiu	764.209		/1949	1966 Sibiu; 19?? Alba Iulia

3–3763 came to Sibiu from the Maramureş Salt Railway in NW Romania; in the early morning of 5 September 1967, it looks splendid as it approaches Mohu with train 2447.
Alfred Luft

Another exile from Maramureş was no. 2–3621 (WrN 3621/1892). Beneşti, 15 September 1966. *Trevor Rowe*

Beneath all the pipework, 399.104 was a Budapest works type 78. Before coming to the CFR in 1944, it had worked for the MÁV (399,104), the ČSD (U34₀₀₂) and the Borzsavölgyi HÉV (23). When photographed at Sibiu on 18 September 1965, it was still carrying a Turda shed plate, suggesting a recent transfer.   *Alfred Luft*

6845 was built by Borsig in 1908 for Huszko, Lozinsky & Co, Kiev. How it reached Romania is unclear, but for many years it worked at Sibiu. 18 September 1965.   *Alfred Luft*

This standard Reşiţa 0–8–0T was the second CFR ng loco to be so numbered, the first being a 1923 Schwartzkopff 0–8–0T. Transferred from industry, 764.109″ worked on the Sibiu system between 1968 and 1972. Agnita, August 1972.
    Antonio Bianco

(4) ALBA IULIA

Company: Gyulafehérvár-Zalatna HÉV

Lines:
Alba Iulia–Zlatna	38km	Opened	11.07.1896
		Regauged	02.05.1984
Zlatna–Valea Dosului	5km	Opened	11.07.1896
			Fr only to serve gold & iron mines at Valea Dosului; abandoned 1984

Apart from the dumped 764.209, visitors to Alba Iulia today would have difficulty in recognising there was once a narrow gauge line here. The line traversed the Valea Ampoiului, SE of the Apuseni mountains, climbing from 218m at Alba Iulia to 402m at Zlatna and 457m at Valea Dosului. Two four-wheel coaches, built by János Weitzer in 1895, are preserved at Zlatna.

Original motive power: *Remarks*

395,001	0–6–2T	StEG	2428/1895	1895–1974 Alba Iulia; wd 1975
395,002			2429/1895	1940 MÁV
395,003			2430/1895	1895–1974 Alba Iulia; wd 1975
395,004			2431/1895	1895–1974 Alba Iulia; wd 1975
395,005		Arad	25/1897	1897–1974 Alba Iulia; wd 1975

Locomotives used after 1960:   *Remarks*

395.104	0–6–2T	KrLi	2360/1890	ex Mori Arco Riva No. 2 'RIVA'; 1945 CFR; 1974 Omaha Zoo Railway, USA, regauged to 980mm
764.201–9	0–8–0	U23A	/1949	c. 1970–1975 3–4 locos Alba Iulia
764.411	0–8–0T	Res	/195?	ex CFI; wd 1981
764.412			/195?	ex CFI; wd 1981
764.413			1323/1957	ex CFI; wd 1981
I.M. ZLATNA 1			1249/1956	wd Zlatna 1988

In 1895 StEG built four of these 0–6–2Ts for the Alba Iulia–Zlatna railway, which opened the following year. Zlatna, 6 October 1969.
Alfred Luft

395.003 (StEG 2430/1895) works a passenger train along the Ampoiului valley near Poiane Ampoiului on 6 October 1969.   Alfred Luft

Some of the standard Reşiţa 0–8–0Ts were allocated to the CFR and, to add to the confusion, had the same numbers as their CFF counterparts; one such was 764.412 with a freight between Şard Ighin and Tăutul Ampoiului. 6 September 1967.
Alfred Luft

János Weitzer of Arad built a mere 131 locomotives and 395.005 (Arad 25/1897) was one of only two which operated on the 760mm lines of the CFR. Zlatna, 14 September 1966.
Trevor Rowe

In a scene which had probably changed little in 70 years, 395.104 (KrLi 2360/1890) hauls an Alba Iulia bound passenger on 6 September 1967. In 1974 the loco was sold to the Omaha Zoo Railway in the USA.
Alfred Luft

(5) TURDA

Company: Torda-Topánfalva-Abrudbányai HÉV

Line: Turda–Abrud 94km Opened 20.06.1912

Unlike the other 760mm lines in Romania, this railway is characterised by several major engineering works in the form of large viaducts and a tunnel as it runs through the Valea Arieşului. The 1965–66 timetable featured a *tren accelerat* (express), uniquely on the CFR narrow gauge.

Original motive power:		*Remarks*
490,007 0–8–0T Bp	2847/1911	1918 SHS 490.007
490,008	2848/1911	1924 CFR
490,009	2849/1911	1924 CFR
490,010	2850/1911	1918 SHS 490.010
490,011	2851/1912	1924 CFR
490,012	2852/1912	1918 CFR
490,013	2853/1912	1918 SHS 490.013
490,014	2854/1912	1918 CFR; wd 1975
490,015	2861/1912	1918 SHS 490.015; 1945 Mariazellerbahn; 1947 JDŽ
490,016	2862/1912	1918 CFR
490,017	2863/1912	1918 CFR; wd 1975

Locomotives used after 1960:		*Remarks*
3797 0–8–0T Bp	3797/1915	ex kkHB 4007; wd 1975
490.021	3154/1914	wd 1974
490.027	3160/1914	wd 1974
490.040	5261/1942	wd 1974
490.043	5264/1942	wd 1974

Abrud station shortly after the opening of the line in 1912.
    Collection: Şerban Lacriţeanu

764.152 works a passenger between Musca and Lupşa on the Turda system on 17 September 1965. (For further photographs of this line, see pages 16, 18 and 22.)   Gerhard Luft

Polish built 764.054 (Chrz 1995/1948) raises steam at Turda. 1 August 1971.   Trevor Rowe

93

764.014		Res	381/1937	
764.054	0–8–0	Chrz	1995/1948	
764.059			2000/1948	pres Turda MPD
764.151	0–8–0T	U23A	/1949	wd 1976
764.152			/1949	
764.154			/1949	wd 1976
764.301		Bors	7831/1910	ex CFF 1960; wd 1975
764.409		Res	1325/1952	ex CFF 1960; wd 1984

(6) ODOBEŞTI

This 23km long line went into the Valea Putnei, from Odobeşti to Burca. It was originally constructed by pioneers of the Deutsche Heeresfeldbahn in World War I to the gauge of 600mm. It was taken over by the CFR after 1918 and regauged to 760mm *c.* 1950. Unfortunately nothing is known about the original motive power.

The line was closed on 25 May 1977 and, unlike the other CFR narrow gauge lines, only ever used steam traction.

Known motive power:

				Remarks
040–I	0–8–0T	O&K	/1925	wd 1974
040–II			/1929	wd 1974
040–3 *(sic)*			/1923	wd 1974
492.001		Bp	2219/1909	ex MÁV; 1945 CFR; wd 1974
764.205	0–8–0	U23A	528/1949	Odobeşti 1976–78
764.392	0–8–0T	Res	1091/1953	ex CFF 1966; 1978 pres Galaţi
764.414			/195?	ex CFI; 1979 pres Tecuci
764.463			1203/1956	ex CFF; 1979 pres Adjud

The most modern locomotives to run on the CFR ng lines were these 0–8–0s, 10 of which were built by the August 23 Works in 1949. 764.201 was photographed shunting at Alba Iulia in August 1975.

Şerban Lacriţeanu

Dieselisation of the CFR 760mm lines took place in the mid 1970s, but many of the postwar steam locos are still in existence. They owe their survival to their use as mobile heating units, often giving the false impression that the train is double-headed by a diesel and a steam loco. 764.155 was preparing for one such duty at Sibiu MPD in the winter of 1991–92. The CFR has recently restored some ng steam locos to working order for special trains. Şerban Lacriţeanu

FROM THE IRON TO THE BAMBOO CURTAIN – A NARROW GAUGE SURVIVOR

Keith Chester, Peeter Klaus & Jeffrey Lanham

Russia is so closely associated with its broad gauge of 1,524mm that it is easy to overlook the fact that extensive use was, and indeed still is, made of narrow gauge lines, usually 750mm. One simple statistic should suffice to emphasise the importance of narrow gauge railways to the Soviet economy: in the 10-year period after 1945 over 5,200 750mm gauge steam locos were built for use in the USSR, whilst the broad gauge lines received approximately 8,500 new locos. As early as the 1880s, Czarist Russia began a programme of standardisation of its locomotive fleet: a tradition that was continued by the Communists after the Revolution of 1917. For a country of its size, both Russia and later the Soviet Union produced relatively few locomotive designs, but those it did were constructed on a scale hardly imaginable anywhere else.

One of the most successful of all of these is the subject of this article: a narrow gauge 0–8–0, built by various manufacturers both within the USSR and abroad between 1941 and *c.* 1987. Given the number of locomotive builders involved it is not surprising to find considerable detail differences amongst the locos which emerged from their factories, though to all intents and purposes the same basic design was adhered to. The class was given a wide variety of designations: P24; PT–4; VP–1/2/4; K^F–4; K^C–4; K^V–4; K^P–4; C2, to name but the most important. These classifications were largely according to the country of

May Day 1949 and Joseph Stalin's portrait sits proudly on the smokebox door of PT–4–088 (Tam 611/1947) as it awaits departure in Tallinn-Väike.   Collection: Peeter Klaus

Between 1903 and 1930, Kolomna built approximately 500 of these light 0–6–0s, class 86, for the Russian, and later the Soviet, armies.
Collection: Peeter Klaus

origin. For convenience here, however, the type will be generally referred to as 'PT–4'. It is estimated that approximately 5,100 'PT–4's were constructed, thus making it easily the largest narrow gauge class ever built anywhere in the world. Moreover many are still in service in China and it is more than likely that they will be one of the last active narrow gauge steam locomotive types in the world.

Between 1903 and 1930 approximately 500 750mm gauge 0–6–0s, with a two-axle tender, were constructed by Kolomna for the *Polevye Zeleznye Dorogi* (= Field Railways of the Imperial Russian Army). These were designated class 86. After 1917 they were widely dispersed (some even found their way to Turkey becoming TCDD 33901–50) and many ended up on narrow gauge industrial lines in the Soviet Union. The rapid industrialisation of the country in the 1920s brought with it a significant increase in the use of narrow gauge railways. This led to the Kolomna Works designing a more powerful replacement for the by now ageing class 86.

Unlike its predecessor, the new 0–8–0T+T (classified as 159) was superheated. Axle loadings were restricted to four tonnes to allow wide availability on the lightly laid Soviet narrow gauge lines; a four-wheel tender was fitted to permit a wide range of operations. In view of the large number of class 86 then still in service, the 159 was so designed as to provide the maximum interchangeability of parts between the two classes; this might account for its rather old-fashioned appearance. Between 1930 and 1941 approximately 1,000 159s were built by four locomotive factories, Kolomna, Podolsk, Novocherkassk and Nevsky. This perhaps suggests strict adherence to a 5-Year Plan rather than any intrinsic worth of the 159 itself. For despite these considerable numbers, the design was not considered a success. The firebox was too small and the degree of superheat inadequate. In service the 159 proved uneconomical.

At the beginning of the 1940s, Kolomna developed a new 0–8–0, class P24 (= works project 24). In effect this was a modernised and more powerful version of the 159. The P24 retained the wheel

In the 1920s many of the 86s were disposed of by the military and worked on various industrial and ng railways throughout old Russia. This view shows T.30 (Kolomna 2669/1903) on the Lavassaare–Pärnu line in Estonia.
  Collection: Peeter Klaus

Fifty class 86 came into the stock of the TCDD and were used on the Sarikamiş–Erzurum line. A few were later transferred to Samsun, where 33929 was photographed in 1970.
  Rod Farr

and cylinder dimensions of the 159, but employed an improved boiler, the diameter of which was increased from 900mm to 1,000mm. To keep axle loadings down to the all-important four tonnes, the side tanks were dispensed with and a larger tender provided. The other obvious change was enclosing the boiler dome and the sandbox within a common casing. The new loco was equipped with a four-row Schmidt superheater and care was taken to ensure that the grate area (the Achille's heel of the 159) was increased. Nominal tractive effort (at 60%) was 3,168kg (6,985lbs). The loco had welded plate frames, 14mm thick. A steam brake was employed on the loco; on the tender a hand-brake.

Nine P24s were built by Kolomna in 1941, but further construction was halted by Hitler's invasion of the Soviet Union in the September of that year. The locos found employment in the peat industry.

The devastation in the western USSR during World War II was enormous and, as elsewhere in Europe, railways were of vital importance to the process of reconstruction. In turn this meant there was a great need for new motive power. After three years in service, it was evident that the P24 was not an entirely satisfactory alternative to the 159. Thus when in 1944–45 the project was revised it was a modified version of the P24 that was developed. This was now classified 'PT–4', whereby:

P = *parowoz* = steam loco
T = *tenderny* = tender
4 = 4 tonne axle loading.

PT–4 LIST
USSR

P24
P24–01 – P24–09
Built Kolomna 1941
P24–07 is Kolo 8225/1941, suggesting the class is Kolo 8219–27/1941.

The class 159 0–8–0T+T was conceived as a replacement for the 86 to provide a modern and powerful loco for the growing number of 750mm lines in the USSR. Unfortunately it was not particularly successful.
Collection: Peeter Klaus

The P24 was a marked improvement on the 159; whilst not entirely satisfactory, it was to form the basis of a family of locos over 5,100 strong. The locos were subsequently rebuilt with a large cabside window.
Collection: Keith Chester

Between 1945 and 1959, large numbers of 'PT–4's under various class designations were constructed both in the USSR itself and in Finland, Czechoslovakia, Hungary and Poland; in the latter cases, they were delivered as either war reparations or were exported on the basis of a commercial order, though, given the relationship of the USSR to these states, it is doubtful whether the Soviets paid the full 'market' price for them. No 'PT–4's, however, were built in either Romania or that part of Germany which was then occupied by the Soviets (subsequently the GDR), despite the existence of well-established locomotive manufacturers

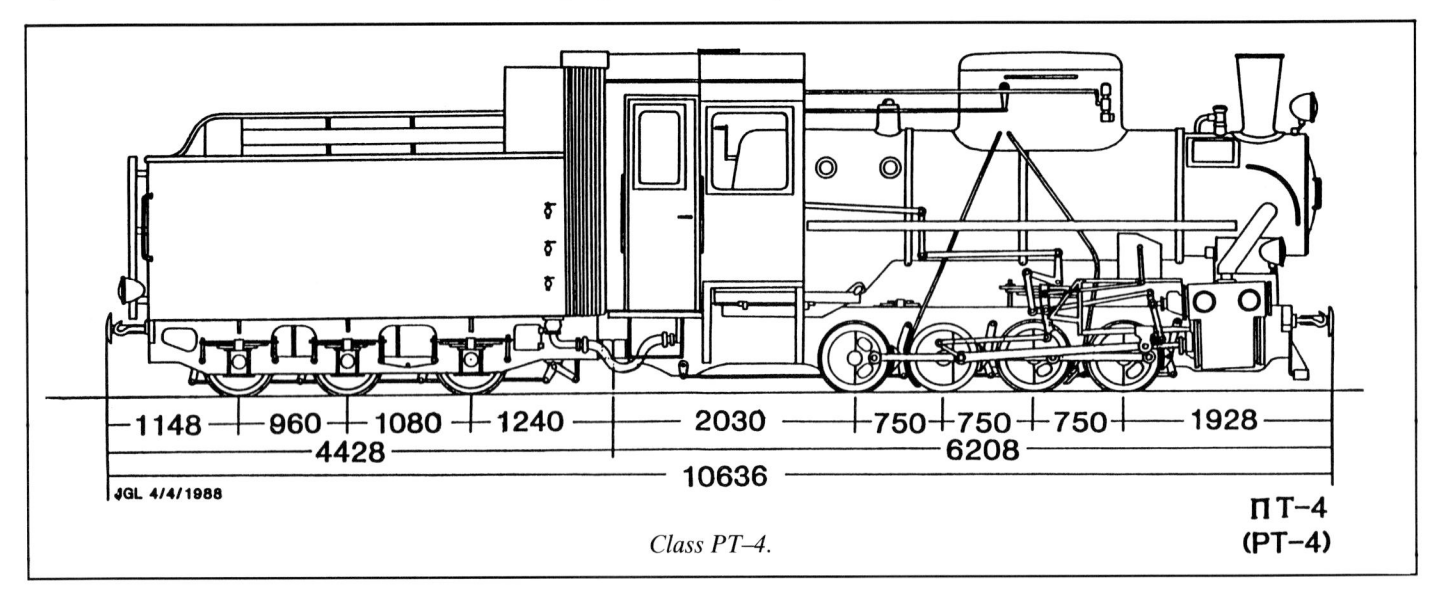

Class PT–4.

PT-4-570 (Tam 871/1951) is steam tested at the Tampella works in 1951.
Collection: Peeter Klaus

PT–4 LIST continued		
FINLAND		
TAMPELLA		
PT–001–035	Tam	574–608/1946
086–122		609–645/1947
139		646/1947
140–1xx		647–6xx/1947
1xx–184		6xx–691/1948
185–193		692–700/1948
269–2xx		701–7xx/1948
2xx–314		7xx–746/1949
315–3xx		747–7xx/1949(?)
3xx–367		7xx–799/1950(?)
368–383		806–821/1950(?)
K^F–4–15–16		822–823/1950(?)
PT–4–384–388		824–828/1951(?)
430–483		829–882/1951(?)
537–570		883–916/1952(?)
K^F–4–17–20		917–920/1952(?)
K^F–4–1–6 = PT–4–431–436		
LOKOMO		
PT–4–036–070	Lokom	223–257/1946
071–085		258–272/1947
123–138		273–288/1947
194–200		289–295/1947
201–236		296–331/1948
237–268		332–363/1949
389–396		364–371/1949
397–423		372–398/1950
K^F–4–7–8		399–400/1950
PT–4–424–426		401–403/1950
K^F–4–9		404/1951
PT–4–427		405/1951
K^F–4–10–14		406–410/1951
PT–4–428–429		411–412/1951
484–512		413–441/1951
513–536		442–465/1952

in both countries. In the case of Romania, it may be speculated that its rather limited locomotive industry was fully occupied with the repair of ex DRB *Kriegsloks* on their way to the Soviet Union as *trofeyny* or booty locos. In addition, it is known that the Soviets were dissatisfied with the workmanship of the Reșița and Malaxa built broad gauge 0–10–0s of type 'Er' and this may also have influenced the decision not to have 'PT–4's manufactured there. Drawings of the P24 were sent to the Orenstein & Koppel works at Babelsberg and the archives at Potsdam record that at the end of September 1946 detail work was being carried out on them; thereafter silence. In the event O&K, renamed LKM Babelsberg in 1948, constructed over 400 'Gr' (= *Germanskaja reparatsia* or German reparations), a very German-looking narrow gauge 0–8–0, especially developed for the Soviet Union.

The first 'PT–4's were built in Finland, which began to deliver reparations to the USSR in mid 1944. The locos built in Finland as reparations were actually designated PT–4. In 1944–45, Lokomo constructed 26 0–4–0Ts (F_L–6) and Tampella 30 0–6–2Ts (F_T–4) for 'Soteva' (Soviet Delegation of War Reparation Industries). Both types were based on older Finnish designs, but with increased water and fuel capacity. For whatever reason (and one may only assume that it was a case of a readily available existing design in a country where war was not raging), Soteva required these locos urgently and this delayed the production of the PT–4 until 1945. Whilst a few more F_L–6s and then twenty (modified) F_L–6s were delivered to Soteva, henceforth all Finnish efforts were concentrated on the large scale manufacture of PT–4s.

The demands for reparations now placed upon the Finns by the Soviets far outstripped the capacity of the individual Finnish locomotive manufacturers: thus boilers were built by Lokomo; Valmet (the state-owned aviation company) supplied the cabs and tenders and Tampella manufactured the rest. It was perhaps fortunate that all three companies were located in Tampere! Both Lokomo and Tampella erected the locomotives. In all, 570 PT–4s were supplied to the USSR as reparations between 1946 and 1952; a further 20 were sold to it in 1950–52 as class K^F–4. The Finnish built PT–4 may be considered as something of an intermediary design, one which made greater use of welding than the P24. The boiler barrel, the smokebox and the firebox were all of welded construction, but the boiler and the firebox were still riveted together. Two types of chimney were fitted: one with a turbine spark arrester (which proved unsatisfactory in service) and a conventional conical one.

Curiously, on the Lokomo GA drawing of PT–4–051, we find 'P24', not 'PT–4', just above the draughtsman's signature. A slip of the pen, or are we to conclude from this that, apart from the increased application of welding, the Finns made very few modifications to the P24? Certainly the fact that the Soviets and later the Czechoslovaks modified the PT–4 design when producing their own versions might suggest that the PT–4 had inherited many of the inherent weaknesses of the P24.

In addition to the PT–4s, the Finns also built diesel locos for the Soviets. Construction on such a large scale was very much at the expense of the domestic market. Between 1945 and 1949, the VR acquired only 18 new locos from Lokomo and Tampella, as opposed to 46 from the USA. Private and industrial railways were likewise forced to import and 10 locos were purchased from Tubize, Couillet and Ducroo & Brauns (the latter diverted from the Dutch East Indies?). Yet large though these orders for locomotives were, they represented but a small proportion of the total reparations sent to the Soviet Union from Finland. In the immediate postwar period this stretched what industry Finland had to its limits, but was ultimately instrumental in turning a predominantly agricultural economy into an industrial one.

In the USSR itself the first of the new 0–8–0s was completed at Votkinsk Works in February 1947. Unlike the PT–4, the boiler was all-welded. Full production did not commence till the following year but from then until 1959 approximately 2,300 locos of this

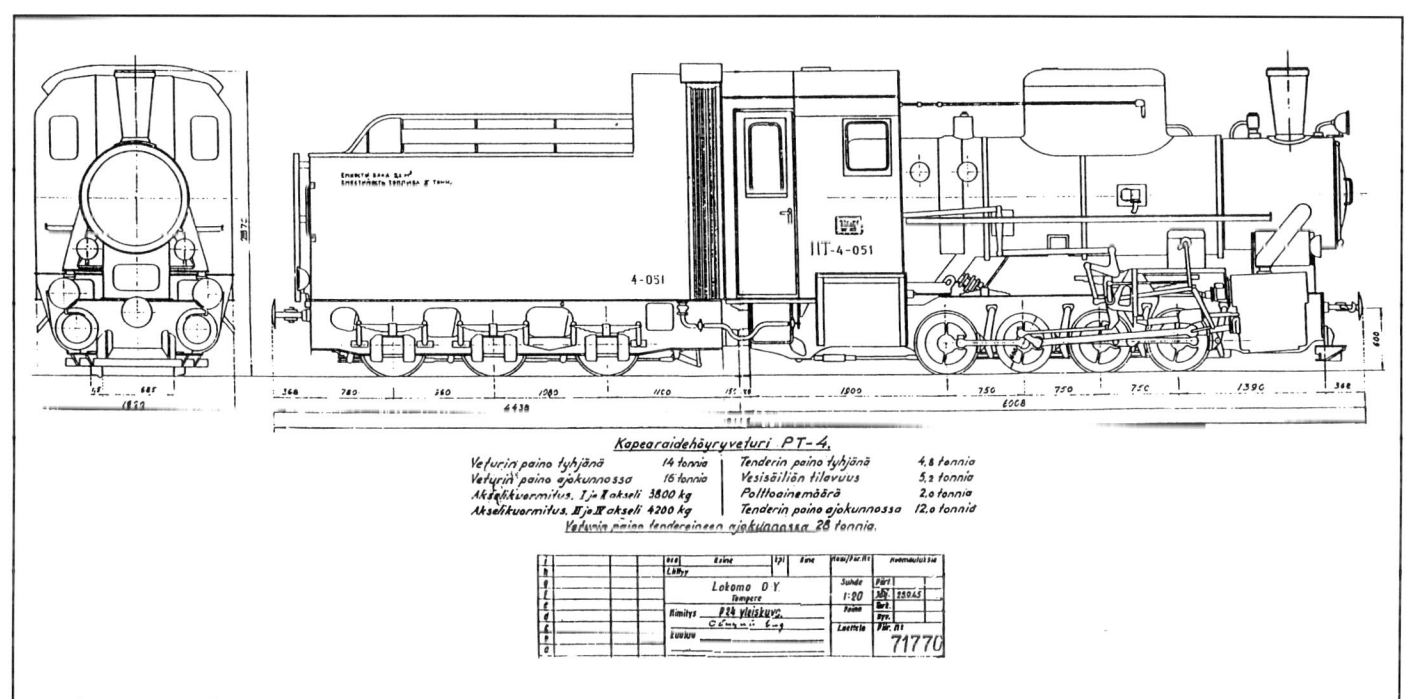

Lokomo general arrangement drawing of PT–4–051; note the small cabside window and the appearance of the designation P24 above the draughtsman's signature. All(?) of the PT–4s received large cabs.

type were constructed. These were divided into three classes, designated VP–1, VP–2 and VP–4. All were to the same basic design, with the classifications reflecting detail differences and improvements, principally to the boiler. These may be summarised as follows:

VP–1: standard boiler

VP–2: new firebox design, without stayrods to the firebox ceiling but with a corrugated wrapper plate

VP–4: until 1954, boiler with standard firebox, but equipped with steam dryer and spark arrester. All VP–4 fitted with airbrakes with a steam pump.

Interestingly, whilst Soviet literature refers to the three classes and these boiler variations, the locos themselves were only observed with VP–1 and VP–4 on their cab sides. The 20mm thick steel corrugated wrapper plate, introduced with the VP–2, simplified the structure of the firebox. It reduced the distortions of the inner firebox wrapper plate and the firebox side sheets could now be secured by rigid staybolts instead of flexible ones. The inner firebox back and side sheets were 11mm thick (10mm on the PT–4). The thickness of the firebox tube sheet was also increased by 2mm to 14mm and that of the front tube sheet from 13mm to 17mm. There were two fusible plugs on the corrugated wrapper plate, one at the front and the other at the rear of the firebox. These changes to the firebox had little effect on the boiler's heating surface, raising it by a mere 0.15–0.2m².

Further minor modifications were made to the VP–1–4s. The electrical system was new and was powered by a TT–1M turbine generator, a standard one used on 1,524mm gauge locos. The force-feed lubricator was also a standard SŽD design and differed from that fitted to the PT–4. Otherwise the most obvious difference between the Soviet built VP (= *Votkinskii Parowoz* or Votkinsk steam loco) series and the Finnish PT–4s, as well as all subsequent variants of the type, was the separated steam and sand dome on top of the boiler; on all the non-Soviet built versions this was combined, as indeed it had been on the P24.

PT–4 LIST *continued*

USSR

VP

VP–1 1948–49 approx. 620 locos

VP–2 1949–54 approx. 400–500 locos

VP–4 1956–59 approx. 1,200–1,300 locos

All built Votkinsk:

A few VP works numbers are known, but they fit no specific pattern. Sometimes the running number repeats the works number (e.g. VP–1–899 is Votsk 899/1951); more often there is no correlation.

Exactly how many ng 0–8–0s the Votkinsk works constructed between 1948 and 1959 remains for the present a mystery. Here an unidentified Vp–1 is seen at work on the Vijshnevolotzkoje peat railway in Russia. Collection: Peeter Klaus

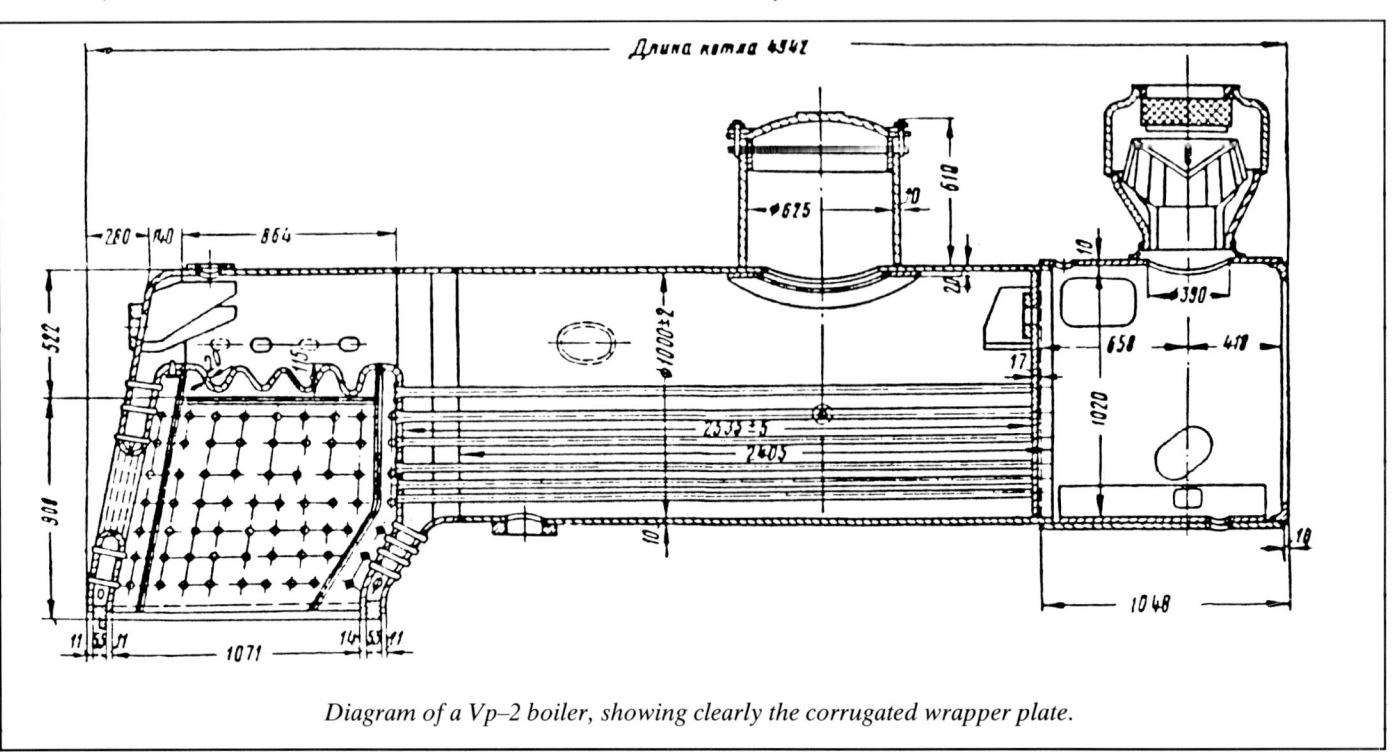

Diagram of a Vp–2 boiler, showing clearly the corrugated wrapper plate.

Vp4–1243 was one of a number of 0–8–0s allocated to the 750mm system of the Maardu chemical works in Estonia. June 1956.
  Collection: Peeter Klaus

PT–4–215 (Lokomo 310/1948) also worked at Maardu. Compare the single dome of the PT–4 with the two separate ones of the Vp.
  Collection: Peeter Klaus

Twin Cylinder Narrow Gauge Locomotive, Series KČ4, for the USSR

To enable this narrow gauge locomotive, which has four coupled axles, to negotiate curves of 40 metres (131ft) of radius the tyres of the third coupled, i.e. the driving axle, have no flange.

The conventional type of boiler with a steel fire box is all-welded except for the junction of the fire box with the cylindrical boiler. It has the usual Schmidt superheater and a valve type throttle.

The frame of the locomotive is made of rolled plates and also all-welded.

The steam engine has a Heusinger valve gear with internal steam inlet and the driving mechanism is designed to have the lightest possible weight.

The locomotive cab is completely enclosed and joined with the tender by means of bellows so that it affords to the crew of the locomotive the greatest comfort even under the most severe climatic conditions.

All piping of the locomotive is well lagged and protected against frost.

The steam brake acts upon all wheels of the locomotive and of the three-axle tender.

This locomotive is the perfect example of a modern narrow-gauge engine manufactured with the most extensive possible application of progressive production methods.

This technical description of the K^C–4, printed in the Škoda catalogue of 1955, may be taken as representative of the PT–4 as a whole.

As Central Europe fell under Soviet control after 1945, its locomotive manufacturers either received large orders for, or were required to deliver as reparations, locomotives of the 'PT–4' design to the USSR.

The first to do so was Czechoslovakia where Škoda of Plzeň constructed 420 'PT–4's for the Soviet Union between 1949 and 1951. (Tenders were supplied by the K. Gottwald works at Brno.) These were numbered K^Č–4 001–420. Note that as with the free trade 'PT–4's from Finland, the designation was changed to K*–4. It is believed that the 'K' showed that the loco was a Kolomna project or design. 'PT–4's manufactured abroad for the USSR now used this new designation of K, plus a sub letter indicating the country of origin. In most cases this is self-evident, save for the MÁVAG locos, where it is a 'V'; this stands for *Vengerskii* (Hungary). Of course these designations were in cyrillic on the locos which went to the USSR. The 4 as always refers to the four tonne axle-loading.

Four Škoda built K^Č–4 remained in Czechoslovakia. Numbered K^Č–4 197–200 (Škoda 2696–99/1950 or 1952), these are said to be duplicate numbers (so why not K^Č–4 1–4?). Three worked at the Prachovice cement works and the fourth, K^Č–4 199, at the iron works at Podbrezová in Slovakia. It was subsequently sold to the forestry railway at Liptovský Hrádok, but is believed never to have seen service there. It is still to be found at Liptovský Hrádok, where it is now preserved.

Kč–4 199 (Škoda 2698/1952) was one of four 0–8–0s which stayed in Czechoslovakia. By July 1969 it was already dumped at Liptovský Hrádok, where today it is preserved.
Jiri Joachymstál

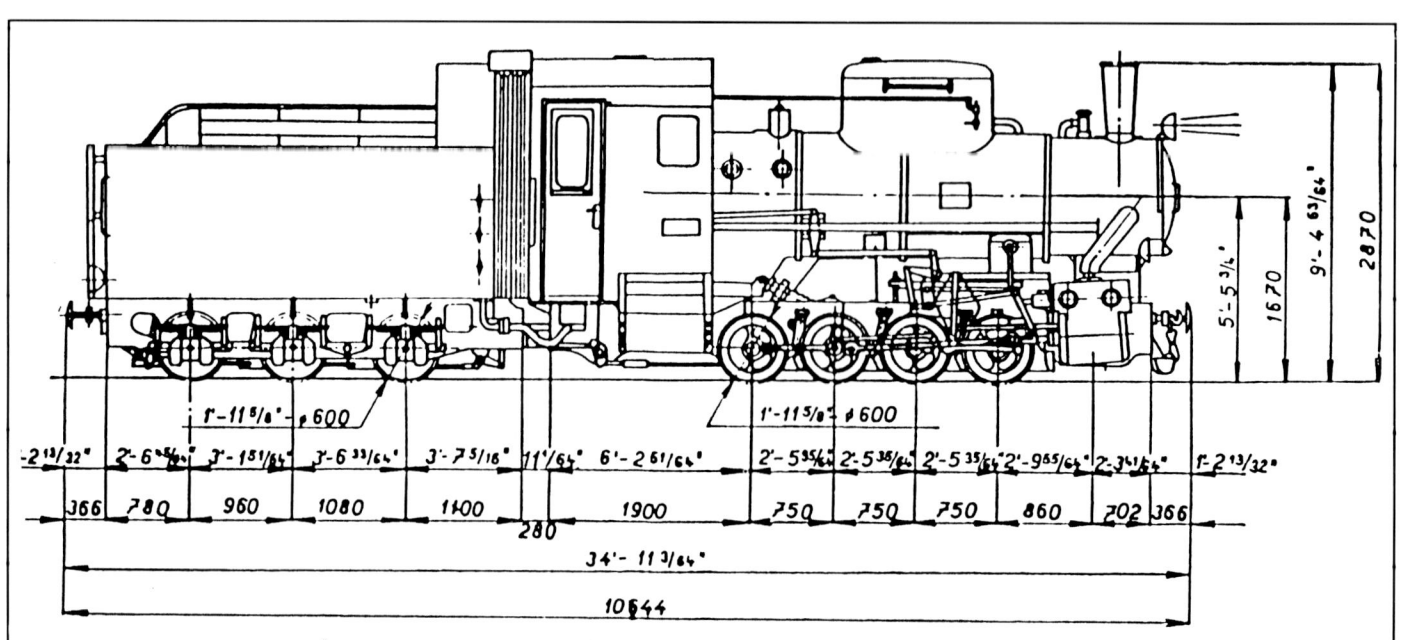

Drawing of a Czech built K^Č–4, taken from the 1955 Škoda catalogue; like the LOKOMO GA drawing, this too shows the loco with the small cabside window, whilst the Škoda locos all had a large window.

The K^Č–4 is featured in the Škoda catalogue of 1955. This uses a photograph of a standard K^Č–4, whilst the accompanying drawing shows a loco with a small cab window, which corresponds to the general arrangement drawing supplied to Finland by the Soviets for the PT–4. As far as is known the whole class was built with the large cab window: so why the difference? The original P24s were all constructed with the small cab window and only later rebuilt with a larger one. Were the Czechoslovaks, like the Finns, initially supplied with the drawings of the P24 and a list of the changes to be made to it? And was this drawing then used in the catalogue? If so, this may explain the apparent discrepancy between the drawing and the locomotives as built.

Whatever the case, by the late 1940s it was evident that all was not well with the PT–4. The Soviets had, in the VP–1–4s, made some modifications to the basic design and the Czechoslovaks were to incorporate a considerable number into the K^Č–4. As the 1957 Chinese Forestry Publishing House handbook on the class notes, 'Later, in response to requests from the customer (Ministry of Forestry and Paper Industry of the USSR), the K^Č–4 steam locomotive was modified. These modifications were made because of the running tests undertaken on the PT–4 locomotives'. These included a whole range of minor modifications, such as a new version of the AVU–6 water feeder (on later locos type AEV), substituting the nap mat in the axle box lubricator with felt filler and so on; there was also an increased use of cast rather than welded components.

reduced, the boiler heating area was decreased by 1.06m^2. Two fusible plugs were fitted on the inner firebox crown sheet – at the front and the rear of the firebox. The PT–4 had only had one and this modification was probably a consequence of the experience gained with the VP–2. It may be assumed that many of these modifications, and others, were incorporated into the K^V–4 and K^P–4, as well as the Chinese built locos.

MÁVAG of Budapest constructed 234 K^V–4 for the USSR between 1950 and 1955. A further six also remained in Hungary where they found employment on various state-owned forestry and agricultural railways. The 1951 MÁVAG catalogue describes the loco as being almost completely of welded construction including the boiler save for a 'double-row riveted seam for joining the boiler . . . and the firebox'. Steam was passed to the cylinders through a 'Tzar' type throttle valve. Unlike the Škoda catalogue, it refers to the tender brakes as being manually operated; great emphasis too is placed on the fact that the loco was intended primarily for wood firing and that the tender was designed with this in mind.

PT–4 LISTS *continued*

CZECHOSLOVAKIA

ŠKODA

K^Č–4–001–167	Škoda	2016–2182/1949
168–343		2183–2358/1950
344–420		2359–2435/1951

Four K^Č–4 remained in Czechoslovakia, with duplicate running numbers:

K^Č–4–197–200	Škoda	2696–2699/1952

On K^Č–4–157 and subsequent locos, three small tubes at the top of the firebox tube sheet were removed. These had overlapped with the curved edge of the grate area, making tube replacement cumbersome. Because the number of small tubes was thus

PT–4 LISTS *continued*

HUNGARY

MÁVAG

K^V–4–001–036	MÁVAG	6235–6270/1950
037–084		6481–6528/1951
085–089		6534–6538/1952
090–144		6539–6593/1953
145–163		6944–6962/1953
164–197		6966–6999/1954
198–201		7001–7004/1954
202–213		7242–7253/1954
214–234		7257–7277/1954

Six K^V–4 remained in Hungary:

G.V.I. 496.075–077	MÁVAG	6963–65/1954
496.078		7255/1954
496.082		7256/1954
A.E.V. 447.401	MÁVAG	7254/1954

G.V.I. = *Gazdasagi Vasutak Igazgatósága* (= Directorate of Agricultural Railways)

A.E.V. = *Allami Erdei Vasutak* (= State Forestry Railways)

K^V–4–156 (MÁVAG 6956/1953) heads a trainload of timber on the Sonda–Mustvee line in eastern Estonia. c. 1965.
Collection: Peeter Klaus

It may be speculated that the Hungarians were not originally intended to receive such a large order. A short paragraph in *The Glasgow Herald* for 3 March 1948 speaks of the Soviets wishing to place a substantial order for locomotives with the North British Locomotive Company; *The Daily Graphic* of the same date reports that the Glasgow company hoped to win an order for 1,100 locos, worth £7,500,000. Although no specific locomotive types are mentioned, it would be reasonable to assume that such an order would have included 'PT–4's. It should be remembered that in the immediate postwar period, Britain's Labour government concluded several trade agreements with its erstwhile wartime ally. By mid 1948, however, the new realities of the cold war were starting to make themselves felt and presumably the order fell foul of the growing mistrust between East and West. In *Russian Steam Locomotives*, (David & Charles 1972), Le Fleming and Price record that the British 'Government were unwilling to provide the necessary export credit and the order was diverted to Hungary'. Further details on this would be welcome.

By far the largest supplier of 'PT–4's outside of the Soviet Union was Fablok of Chrzanów in Poland. Between 1950 and 1959, it is believed to have delivered 790 K^P–4s to the USSR and 81 to China in 1950–52. Ten are said to have been supplied to North Korea; some sources state these were transferred from China, others that they were a direct delivery with Chrzanów works numbers 3030–39/1952.

The tenders were supplied by Pafawag and boilers by Cegielski, Warszawa and Sosnowiec. These were the first welded boilers built in Poland.

Twenty K^P–4s remained in Poland (apparently as the result of cancelled orders), where they worked on various forestry and sugar beet railways. The final one in regular service was Chrz 3762/1957 at Ostrowite sugar factory where it is said to have last worked during the 1988–89 campaign.

Twenty of the Chrzanów built Kp–4s worked in Poland, principally at sugar factories and on forestry railways. CK 1 (Chrz 3761/1957) is seen here with a train of sugar beets at Konavy. October 1985.
Helmut Pochadt

CK 2 (Chrz 3772/1957) shunts wagons of beets at Kruszwica Sugar Factory in central Poland on 3 October 1981. Maciej Matuszewski

PT–4 LISTS continued

POLAND

CHRZANÓW

K^P–4–001–120	Chrz	2281–2400/1950
121–177		2401–2457/1952
		3360–3389/1957
		3660–3707/1957
		3709–3759/1957
		3763–3770/1957
		3774–3777/1957
		3779–3789/1957
		3890–3958/1957
		4290–4399/1958
		4782–4899/1958
		5029–5030/1959
		5051–5072/1959

NB. No complete list of Chrzanów locos exists and the one above needs to be treated with considerable caution. K^P–4–469, for example, was recorded with worksplate Chrz 4384/1955. Moreover it accounts for only 738 locos, whereas 790 K^P–4 are supposed to have been delivered to the USSR. The question arises whether this number was actually built.

Exported direct to China:

Chrz 2458–2545/1950(?)

Exported to North Korea (direct or via China?):

Chrz 3030–3039/1952(?)

The following K^P–4 remained in Poland:

Chrz 3390/1957	Kp4–1255	(ZKL Cisna)
3708/1957	Kp4–1256	(ZKL Cisna)
3760/1957	3	(Cukr. Goslawice; after 1975 Cukr. Dobre 4″)
3761/1957	CK 1	(Cukr. Kruszwica)
3762/1957	CO 1	(Cukr. Ostrowite)
3772/1957	CK 2	(Cukr. Kruszwica)
3773/1957	CBK 12	(Cukr. Brześć–Kujawski; later CBK 6″)
3778/1957	CBK 13	(Cukr. Brześć–Kujawski; later CBK 5″)
3779/1957	—	(Kopalnia Pirytu 'Staszic', Rudki)
3790/1957	Kp4–1257	(ZKL Cisna)
3791/1957	Kp4–1258	(ZKL Cisna)
3792/1957	CO 2	(Cukr. Ostrowite)
3793/1957	Kp4–1259	(ZKL Cisna)
3794/1957	Kp4–1260	(ZKL Cisna)
4944/1958	—	(Cukr. Opole Lubelskie)
4945/1958	—	(Zaklady Górnicz-Hutnicze 'Sabinów'; 1967 to Stąporków)
5027/1959	—	(Zaklady Górnicz-Hutnicze 'Sabinów'; 1967 to Stąporków)
5028/1959	—	(Zaklady Górnicz-Hutnicze 'Sabinów'; 1967 to Stąporków)
5096/1959	—	(Kopalnia Pirytu 'Staszic', Rudki)

NB. One K^P–4 remains unaccounted for.

As well as the boiler variations mentioned above, there were other detail differences to be found. The Soviet built VPs and the Finnish PT–4s had tenders fitted with SKS roller bearings, whilst those of all other manufacturers used standard plain or sleeve bearings. All the VPs, PT–4s and approximately the first 200 K$^\check{C}$–4s were equipped with a new type of connecting and side rod bearings; the remaining K$^\check{C}$–4s, plus the K^V–4s and K^P–4s had a standard type.

When delivered, there was some considerable variation in livery, to some extent giving the lie to the cold war cliché of the uniform drabness of the USSR. These may be summarised as follows:

PT–4:   green loco and tender, black smokebox, red wheels and green frames (i.e. standard VR livery)

VP: tender and cab green, black boiler, red and white wheels and red frames

K$^\check{C}$–4 etc: black livery with red wheels and frames.

After overhaul, most locos were painted in a plain black livery, though locally some retained their original schemes.

In all something approaching 4,500 'PT–4's were built in, or delivered to, the Soviet Union; because of the uncertainty of the numbers constructed by Votkinsk, it is impossible to put a precise figure to this. Of these 4,500, some found their way to narrow gauge lines operated by the SŽD, but the great majority were used throughout the USSR (and Mongolia) wherever there was a narrow gauge industrial line with light axle loadings, in particular on logging and peat railways. Virtually all of them had been replaced by diesels by the early 1970s. A strategic reserve was maintained for another 10 years or so, after which many were finally scrapped. A small number were sent direct to Pioneer Railways in the 1950s, where some still work. Today about 25 'PT–4's are preserved throughout the former Soviet Union.

Most 'PT–4's had been withdrawn in the USSR by the early 1970s, though many remained in store or dumped long after that. Vp4–1171 will clearly never run again. Novosjolovo, January 1991.

Collection: Peeter Klaus

An interesting question, but one which is now never likely to be resolved, is just exactly how many 'PT–4's were imported into China, and when. Certainly the only direct delivery was that of the 81 (Chrz 2458–2545/1950–52) from Poland. Very few locos in China still carry worksplates, but enough do to suggest that China also received some 'PT–4's from the Soviet Union. The staff at Chaihe claim to have had a Czechoslovak (i.e. Škoda) loco. To date three Chrzanów locos have been confirmed; whilst 2458/1952 at Langxiang clearly belongs to the original delivery, 3840/1959 at Hunjiang and 3849/1959 at Dunhua do not. A MÁVAG loco (6573/1952) has been discovered at Tieli with a cyrillic worksplate, which again would suggest prior use in the USSR. Sino–Soviet relations were very close in the 1950s and the Soviets provided considerable technical assistance of all kinds. In connection with this, it is generally believed that the Chinese received a complete package of forestry railway equipment in the period 1950–60, which would have presumably included locomotives.

It may also be reasonably assumed that 'knowhow' was supplied as well and that along with this came plans for the 'PT–4'. Certainly, the Chinese general arrangement drawing for these 0–8–0s is the same as that of the Finnish built PT–4. Exactly when is unknown but sometime towards the end of the 1950s, the Chinese started building their own version of the 'PT–4'. Two factories in particular, Harbin and Shijiazhuang, were involved in this and their products were classified C2. Interestingly the Chinese language C2 manual calls it type Kn–4 (= K^P–4). This is perhaps not so surprising if, as is probable, the original manual came from Poland with the 1950–52 delivery; in addition it is believed that Fablok not only sent documentation to the Chinese, but also helped them organise the locomotive works at Shijiazhuang and supplied tools and machinery to equip it. The apparent Russian designation (i.e. the use of cyrillic) may be explained by the 'Sovietisation' of all assistance to China in this period.

Some C2s were also built at other factories and, although they often received different classifications (e.g. ZG, B1, YJ or ZM–4), they all conformed to the basic 'PT–4' design. Although presumably initially introduced into China with forestry railways in mind, these useful little engines also quickly established themselves on all types of local, industrial and mineral narrow gauge lines throughout the country. When enthusiasts began exploring such lines in the early 1980s, these 0–8–0s were the first type found on the 762mm gauge lines.

The early history of C2 construction in China is not available partly because foreigners were not able to visit China at this period and also because even today records (assuming they still exist) remain closed. Furthermore identification of the original 'PT–4' (i.e. European built) and the Chinese C2 is often now almost impossible, partly because of the previously mentioned problem of worksplates and partly because constant rebuilding and modification over the past 30 years have rendered many 'PT–4's and C2s virtually indistinguishable.

Surviving examples of the C2 without rebuilding show that they are almost identical to the 'PT–4' except for two significant features. All the C2 type noted so far are fitted with Chinese boilers which have external regulator linkage operating the regulator via a crank and gland on the right hand side of the dome; on the 'PT–4' control is via an internal regulator shaft from the backplate of the boiler to below the dome. The original version of the 'PT–4' has the smokebox extending slightly ahead of the front buffer beam; on all the C2s observed the buffer beam is a little in front of the smokebox. This would seem a sensible modification for locos intended for use on forestry railways and needing to propel logging bogies carrying overhanging timber.

The C2 is normally coal fired and, like the 'PT–4', has a superheated boiler. The cylinders are fitted with piston valves actuated by Walschaerts valve gear. Plate frames are employed with simple springing and equalising. The detail variations which are readily identifiable are as follows:

Cabs: C2s built at Harbin or Shijiazhuang have a cab wider and longer than the original 'PT–4' copy. They are easily recognised by the double side window with the cab extending outside the tender width which allows a small rear window. The total locomotive length is increased from 10,636mm to 10,944mm to make provision for the longer cab and to move the buffer beam forward of the smokebox. Older models may have the smaller single side window cab which is the same width as the tender, the class YJ at Qianmotou and some of the C2s at Ganzhou have this type of cab. Other locos have been noted with the cab widened at the waistline and B*10154 at Dashitou is so fitted, as are 09.B1 002 at Huangnihe and ZG 301 at Kaifeng. On the Yingde Mineral Railway at Goncun in Guangdong there is a C2 (no. 51) with a circular front window and a non-standard tender carrying a 1963 Shijiazhuang plate. It is not possible to define these variations in terms of builders or type variations and no groups seem exactly the same.

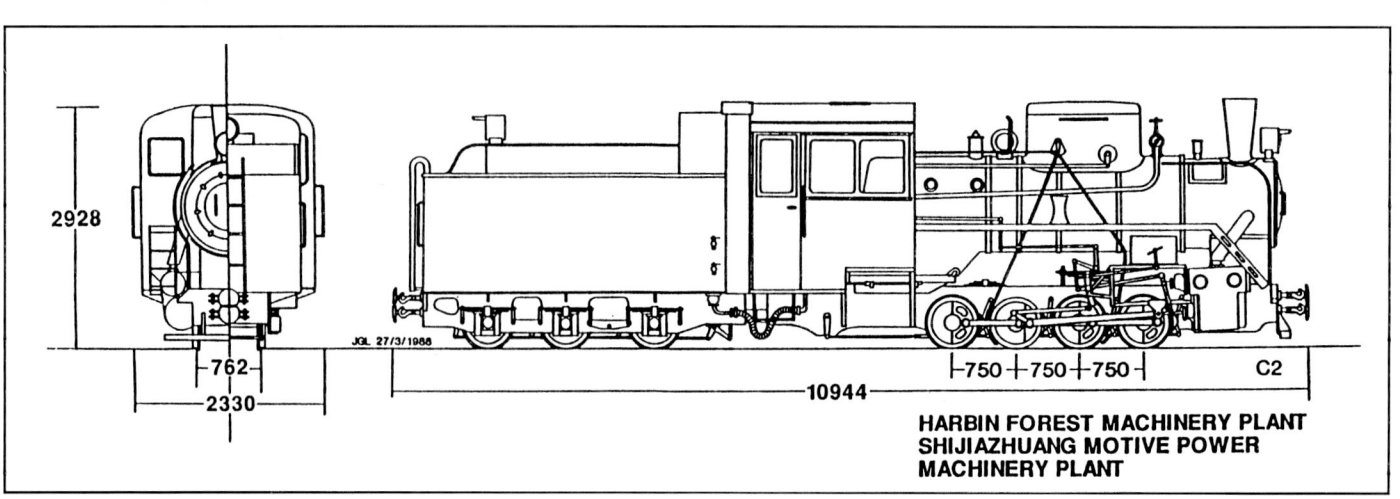

HARBIN FOREST MACHINERY PLANT
SHIJIAZHUANG MOTIVE POWER MACHINERY PLANT

01–B171 on the Lingjiang Forestry Railway is an intermediate Chinese built C2 with a wide cab top and a short cab.   Jeffrey Lanham

658 represents one of the final versions of the C2; it is additionally fitted with automatic couplers, an air pump and reservoir. Hunjiang Mineral Railway.   Jeffrey Lanham

Boilers: The principal boiler differences have already been described save for the final batches, which emerged from Harbin works with the (unlicensed) Chinese version of the Giesl oblong ejector as did some rebuilds.

Tenders: The majority seem to be a 'standard' six-wheel design, but some modifications have been observed, notably the removal of the tender cab with the loco cab altered to suit. Examples of this were to be found at Yingde and Lojiace. However, quite a number have been noted in the last two or three years paired with bogie tenders, similar in size and shape to those of the C4 class 0–8–0s. Some forestry and provincial railways have 'mainlines' of surprising length and this presumably is the explanation for the larger tenders. Bogie tenders are in use at Suileng and on the Xuchang Provincial Railway; an odd example (C2 040) has also been seen at Xinqing.

Couplings: One significant peculiarity of the forestry locomotives is the provision of two centre buffers placed one above the other with side chains for coupling. This arrangement was presumably to allow for rolling stock with buffers at different centres, though in recent years the lower buffer has been removed on some lines. Local and industrial railways utilise either automatic couplings or link and pin couplers. The locos at Hunjiang use what seem to be standard gauge knuckle couplers, which are large for a narrow gauge loco.

Detail variations: These are almost too many to list but the large smoke deflectors fitted to the 'tourist' engine 11042 at Xinqing and the semi-streamlined smoke deflectors carried on the top of the boiler and faired into the dome on the locomotives at Huangnihe are worth mentioning as are the extended front frames (a shunter's platform?) on YJ2809 at Qianmotou. Other noteworthy variations are the positioning of the mechanical lubricators above or below the running plate and the provision, or lack of provision, of steps up to the running plate. The forestry locomotives do not have automatic train brakes but the local and industrial ones often carry air pumps and reservoirs.

As with the Soviet built Vp–1, it is almost impossible to provide accurate figures on the number of C2s constructed in China. Over the years, for example, officials at Harbin have quoted various production figures of 1,000, 500, 220 or about 10 C2s a year for their works. For their part, builders plates offer few clues: none of the Harbin locos seem to carry any plates at all; those built at Shijiazhuang which do have plates appear to include numbers of other construction, as they often seem far too high to be exclusively C2; finally, as already mentioned, many C2/'PT–4's in China have no plates whatsoever. Indeed, in this vast (and still very secretive) country, it is still not known how many plants actually participated in the manufacture of C2s. Nor can we look to the running numbers of the locos in service for any assistance – these have to date defied any attempt to fit them into any recognisable pattern. Our estimate (based on a calculation of 36 forestry railways with 12–15 locos each and a further 200 on provincial and industrial lines) is that approximately 600–650 C2/'PT–4's (and variants) have operated in China. Of these, probably about 500 were actually constructed there, with the locos imported directly from Poland and indirect imports from the USSR accounting for the rest. Of the Chinese built locos, we believe that 200+ and 250+ emerged from the Harbin and Shijiazhuang works respectively. If anything, these are conservative estimates, as it is by no means certain that every 762mm line operating in China over the past 30 years has yet been accounted for.

Construction of C2s ceased in 1987–88 and it seems unlikely that further examples will be built. There has been a steady contraction of 762mm kilometerage in China in recent years, which probably means there are surplus locos available. In addition, Harbin works has also given up the repair of steam locos (indeed it is now reported to be manufacturing buses) which does little to secure the long-term future of steam operated narrow gauge lines, and hence C2s, in China.

The authors would like to acknowledge the assistance of Reino Kalliomäki and Mike Yeoman, as well as the staff of KCRC, in the preparation of this article.

0 1043, a Tieli based C2, receives a major overhaul at the Harbin Forest Machinery Factory in northern China on 28 December 1987.

Robert Koch

'PT–4' type 0–8–0s known to have been built or worked in China

Cab side	Builder	CN	Date	Saddle	SB Plate	Tender	Line
C2–0 1023				1023	B*031023		Tieli, Heilongjiang
C2–0 1043							Tieli, Heilongjiang
Z$_1$3 01044	MÁVAG	6573	1952	44			Tieli, Heilongjiang
C2–0 B3 1067							Tieli, Heilongjiang
C2–0 1047							Tieli, Heilongjiang
C2–0 1049							Tieli, Heilongjiang
B3 1043	Shijiazhuang						Tieli, Heilongjiang
B3 1069							Tieli, Heilongjiang
C2–01023							Tieli, Heilongjiang
C2–010145	Harbin						Tieli, Heilongjiang
1037							Tieli, Heilongjiang
1046							Tieli, Heilongjiang
1048							Tieli, Heilongjiang
1049							Tieli, Heilongjiang
1050	Shijiazhuang	395	1963				Tieli, Heilongjiang
1051							Tieli, Heilongjiang
1052							Tieli, Heilongjiang
1066							Tieli, Heilongjiang
12							Shuangzihe
13							Shuangzihe
14							Shuangzihe
15							Shuangzihe
16							Shuangzihe

*The front end of B*031023. The characters around the smokebox door read 'Realise the Four Modernisations', whilst those in the centre say 'North Wind'. Tieli, 12 April 1986.* Roger Gillard

'PT–4' type 0–8–0s known to have been built or worked in China *continued*

Cab side	Builder	CN	Date	Saddle	SB Plate	Tender	Line
17							Shuangzihe
18							Shuangzihe
19							Shuangzihe
020							Shuangzihe
21							Shuangzihe
22							Shuangzihe
23							Shuangzihe
24							Shuangzihe
25							Shuangzihe
11003	Shijiazhuang	355					Xinqing, Heilongjiang
11009	Shijiazhuang	398 or 396	1963				Xinqing, Heilongjiang
11032							Xinqing, Heilongjiang
11041	Shijiazhuang	389	1963				Xinqing, Heilongjiang
11042	Shijiazhuang	407	1963				Xinqing, Heilongjiang
11043	Shijiazhuang	003	1964				Xinqing, Heilongjiang
11045	Shijiazhuang	007	1964				Xinqing, Heilongjiang
009							Xinqing, Heilongjiang
021							Xinqing, Heilongjiang
028							Xinqing, Heilongjiang
036							Xinqing, Heilongjiang
040							Xinqing, Heilongjiang
011022							Xinqing, Heilongjiang
011014							Xinqing, Heilongjiang
C2–024							Xinqing, Heilongjiang
014	frames only						Xinqing, Heilongjiang
021	frames only						Xinqing, Heilongjiang

026, a Shijiazhuang built C2, leaves Langxiang with a train of empties. 13 January 1988.   Roger Gillard

'PT–4' type 0–8–0s known to have been built or worked in China *continued*

Cab side	Builder	CN	Date	Saddle	SB Plate	Tender	Line
101							Lojiaci, Guangdong
020							Lojiaci, Guangdong
196							Lojiaci, Guangdong
011							Lojiaci, Guangdong
02							Youhao I, Heilongjiang
015							Youhao I, Heilongjiang
014							Youhao II, Heilongjiang
015							Youhao II, Heilongjiang
21							Youhao II, Heilongjiang
064							Youhao II, Heilongjiang
018							Youhao I or II, Heilongjiang
01							Youhao I or II, Heilongjiang
04							Youhao I or II, Heilongjiang
06							Youhao I or II, Heilongjiang
07							Youhao I or II, Heilongjiang
08							Youhao I or II, Heilongjiang
09							Youhao I or II, Heilongjiang
10	Shijiazhuang	001	1964				Youhao I or II, Heilongjiang
—	Harbin	202	1987				Colliery near Beijing
50005	Harbin	new	1987				—
50007	Harbin	new	1987				—
50010	Harbin	new	1987				—
—	Harbin	new	1986				Beifang Mine, Hunan
—	Harbin	new	1986				Beifang Mine, Hunan
—	Harbin	new	1986				Sichuan Province
—	Harbin	new	1986				Sichuan Province

On the Langxiang Forestry Railway, 031 hauls a train of logs out of Jianshe on 12 January 1988. Roger Gillard

'PT–4' type 0–8–0s known to have been built or worked in China *continued*

Cab side	Builder	CN	Date	Saddle	SB Plate	Tender	Line
—	Harbin	new	1986				Chang Chun Brick Factory
—	Harbin	new	1986				Chang Chun Brick Factory
007							At Harbin for repair 1987
05							At Harbin for repair 1987
02							At Harbin for repair 1987
202							At Harbin for repair 1987
2003							At Harbin for repair 1987
12048							At Harbin for repair 1987
B 031005							Shan He Tun
21026							Hua Nan
203							Zhanhe
2007							Tongbei
(31)506							Shan He Tun
195							Zhanhe
YL/04 003							Ar Shan
4011							Ar Shan
21055							Weihe
128							Tian Qiaoling
218							Tian Qiaoling
053							Suileng, Heilongjiang
203							Suileng, Heilongjiang
027							Suileng, Heilongjiang
025							Suileng, Heilongjiang
021							Suileng, Heilongjiang
024							Suileng, Heilongjiang
020							Suileng, Heilongjiang
201							Suileng, Heilongjiang
12							—
2							Jinan Ironworks
B$_1$ 10174							Wang Qing
B 110166							Wang Qing
10134							Wang Qing
5001							Dong Fang Hong
Z6 01009							Changting
Z6 011005							Changting
Z6 011006							Changting
Z6 011010							Changting
Z6 011011							Changting
Z6 011012							Changting
Z6 011016							Changting
ZG 301							Kaifeng
ZG 302							Kaifeng
ZG 303							Kaifeng
309							Ganzhou-Shangyou, Jiangxi
06							Ganzhou-Shangyou, Jiangxi
08							Ganzhou-Shangyou, Jiangxi
22							Ganzhou-Shangyou, Jiangxi
32							Ganzhou-Shangyou, Jiangxi
56							Ganzhou-Shangyou, Jiangxi
65							Ganzhou-Shangyou, Jiangxi
75							Ganzhou-Shangyou, Jiangxi

'PT–4' type 0–8–0s known to have been built or worked in China continued

Cab side	Builder	CN	Date	Saddle	SB Plate	Tender	Line
YJ 2809							Quianmotou-Raoyang
YJ 2813							Quianmotou-Raoyang
YJ 2815							Quianmotou-Raoyang
YJ 2816							Quianmotou-Raoyang
YJ 2817							Quianmotou-Raoyang
YJ 2818							Quianmotou-Raoyang
01							Xilin
02							Xilin
06							Xilin
01							Chaihe, Heilongjiang
02							Chaihe, Heilongjiang
$Z_1 6\ 02101$							Chaihe, Heilongjiang
105							Chaihe, Heilongjiang
Z6 02106							Chaihe, Heilongjiang
Z6 02109							Chaihe, Heilongjiang
Z6 02108							Chaihe, Heilongjiang
110							Chaihe, Heilongjiang
111							Chaihe, Heilongjiang
02112							Chaihe, Heilongjiang
113							Chaihe, Heilongjiang
117							Chaihe, Heilongjiang
119							Chaihe, Heilongjiang
121							Chaihe, Heilongjiang
2122							Chaihe, Heilongjiang
120							Chaihe, Heilongjiang
102							Chaihe, Heilongjiang

Many Chinese forestry railways operate pasenger services. Here 1052 and 169 depart from Wuha with the down passenger on the Tieli system. 12 April 1986.   *Roger Gillard*

'PT–4' type 0–8–0s known to have been built or worked in China *continued*

Cab side	Builder	CN	Date	Saddle	SB Plate	Tender	Line
103							Chaihe, Heilongjiang
104							Chaihe, Heilongjiang
107	Shijiazhuang						Chaihe, Heilongjiang
109							Chaihe, Heilongjiang
115	Shijiazhuang						Chaihe, Heilongjiang
118							Chaihe, Heilongjiang
654							Hunjiang, Jilin
655	Shijiazhuang						Hunjiang, Jilin
656							Hunjiang, Jilin
657							Hunjiang, Jilin
658							Hunjiang, Jilin
659							Hunjiang, Jilin
660	Shijiazhuang	007	1984				Hunjiang, Jilin
662	Chrzanów	3840	1959				Hunjiang, Jilin
663						Pafawag 02500/1958	Hunjiang, Jilin
664							Hunjiang, Jilin
665							Hunjiang, Jilin
01–B102							Lingjiang, Jilin
01–B103							Lingjiang, Jilin
01–B104							Lingjiang, Jilin
01–B105				105			Lingjiang, Jilin
01–B107							Lingjiang, Jilin
01–B108					B_1*108		Lingjiang, Jilin
01–B111				111			Lingjiang, Jilin
01–B171	Shijiazhuang	386	1963				Lingjiang, Jilin
01–B180					B_1*10180		Lingjiang, Jilin
208							Lingjiang, Jilin
1							Heihe
2							Heihe
3							Heihe
4							Heihe
101							Chaihe
104							Chaihe
106							Chaihe
112							Chaihe
120							Chaihe
B1 10149							Dashitou, Jilin
B1 10150							Dashitou, Jilin
B1 10151							Dashitou, Jilin
B1 10152							Dashitou, Jilin
B1 10153							Dashitou, Jilin
B1 10154 (Giesl)							Dashitou, Jilin
B1 10155							Dashitou, Jilin
B1 10156							Dashitou, Jilin
B1 10169							Dashitou, Jilin
B1 10200							Dashitou, Jilin
2							Langxiang, Heilongjiang
22	Harbin						Langxiang, Heilongjiang
24	Shijiazhuang						Langxiang, Heilongjiang
26	Shijiazhuang						Langxiang, Heilongjiang
27	Shijiazhuang						Langxiang, Heilongjiang
27	Harbin						Langxiang, Heilongjiang
28						Pafawag 1067/1952	Langxiang, Heilongjiang
29							Langxiang, Heilongjiang
30	Chrzanów	2458	1952				Langxiang, Heilongjiang

'PT–4' type 0–8–0s known to have been built or worked in China *continued*

Cab side	Builder	CN	Date	Saddle	SB Plate	Tender	Line
31	Harbin						Langxiang, Heilongjiang
33							Langxiang, Heilongjiang
34	Shijiazhuang						Langxiang, Heilongjiang
К п 4 2814							Gao Pei Din Provincial Rly, Hebei
К п 4 2826							Gao Pei Din Provincial Rly, Hebei
К п 4 2814	Shijiazhuang						Gao Pei Din Provincial Rly, Hebei
51	Shijiazhuang	—	1963				Yingde, Guangdong
B1 10109	Shijiazhuang						Dunjua, Jilin
B1 10138							Dunjua, Jilin
B1 10139						Pafawag 0964/1952	Dunjua, Jilin
B1 10140							Dunjua, Jilin
B1 10141							Dunjua, Jilin
B1 10142						Pafawag 0968/1952	Dunjua, Jilin
B1 10143							Dunjua, Jilin
B1 10144							Dunjua, Jilin
10168							Dunjua, Jilin
B1 10178							Dunjua, Jilin
B1 10199							Dunjua, Jilin
B1 10204							Dunjua, Jilin
10205							Dunhua, Jilin
701							Nanyang Provincial Rly

1046 hauls a heavy train of logs out of Wuha for Tieli on 12 April 1986. *Roger Gillard*

'PT–4' type 0–8–0s known to have been built or worked in China *continued*

Cab side	Builder	CN	Date	Saddle	SB Plate	Tender	Line
ZM4							Taiyuan Steel Works
ZM4							Taiyuan Steel Works
Кп4–1							Handan to Dunhua for spares
Кп4 010							Handan to Dunhua for spares
Кп4 —	frames only						Handan to Dunhua for spares
Кп4 —	frames only						Handan to Dunhua for spares
Кп4 —	Chrzanów	3849	1959				Handan to Dunhua for spares
09.B1 001 (10145)							Huangnihe, Jilin
09.B1 002 (10147)						Pafawag 0967/1952	Huangnihe, Jilin
09.B1 003 (10148)							Huangnihe, Jilin
09.B1 004 (10157)							Huangnihe, Jilin
09.B1 005 (101121)							Huangnihe, Jilin
09.B1 006 (10124)							Huangnihe, Jilin
09.B1 007 (10162)							Huangnihe, Jilin
09.B1 008 (10163)							Huangnihe, Jilin
09.B1 009 (10146)							Huangnihe, Jilin
09.B1 010 (10192)							Huangnihe, Jilin
218							Tianqiaoling, Jilin
class C6 2832							—

Shijiazhuang works plate of 0 01023, Tieli, 12 April 1986.
Roger Gillard

Principal Dimensions of 'PT–4' type 0–8–0s

		159	P24	PT–4	VP–1	$K^{\acute{C}}$–4	K^V–4	K^P–4	C2 (early version)	C2 (later version)
LOCO	Gauge	750mm	750mm	750mm	750mm	750mm	750mm	750mm / 762mm	762mm	762mm
	Cylinders bore	285mm	285mm	285mm	285mm	286mm	285mm	285mm	280mm	285mm
	Cylinders stroke	300mm	300mm	300mm	300mm	300mm	300mm	300mm	300mm	300mm
	Driving wheel diameter	600mm	600mm	600mm	600mm	600mm	600mm	600mm	600mm	600mm
	Boiler pressure	13atm	13atm	13atm	13atm	13atm	13atm	13atm	13atm	13atm
	Grate area	$0.718m^2$	$1.01m^2$	$1.01m^2$	$1.01m^2$	$1.01m^2$	$1.02m^2$	$1.01m^2$	$1.01m^2$	$1.01m^2$
	Weight in w/o	16t	16t	16t	16t	16t	16t	16t	—	—
	Power	100hp	175hp	175hp	175hp	175hp	175hp	175hp	250hp	250hp
	Overall height	2870mm	2870mm	2870mm	2870mm	2870mm	2870mm	2870mm	2870mm	2928mm
	Overall width	1900mm	1920mm	1920mm	—	—	—	2060mm	2025mm	2320mm
	Max. speed	30kph	35kph	35kph	35kph	35kph	35kph	35kph	35kph	35kph
	Min. radius curve	—	40m	40m	40m	40m	40m	40m	40m	40m
TENDER	Coal capacity	0.8t	2.0t	2.0t	2.0t	2.0t	2.0t	2.0t	2.0t	2.0t
	Wood capacity	$2.0m^3$	$5.0m^3$	$5.0m^3$	$5.0m^3$	$5.0m^3$	$5.0m^3$	$5.0m^3$	—	—
	Water capacity	$3.5m^3$	$5.2m^3$	$5.2m^3$	$5.2m^3$	$5.2m^3$	$5.2m^3$	$5.2m^3$	$5.2m^3$	$5.2m^3$
	Weight in w/o	8.0t	12t	12t	12t	12t	12t	12t	—	—
LOCO & TENDER	Overall length	9420mm	10446mm	10446mm	10618mm	10644mm	10636mm	10636mm	10636mm	10944mm
	Total weight in w/o	24t	28t	28t	28t	28t	28t	28t	28t	28t